i

Human Resources Flexibilities and Authorities in the Federal Government

U.S. Office of Personnel Management
1900 E. St., NW
Washington DC

This page intentionally left blank.

Preface

This handbook summarizes the major human resources (HR) flexibilities and authorities in the Federal Government and is intended as a reference material for managers, supervisors, and employees on personnel matters dealing with recruiting, retaining, and motivating the Federal workforce. These HR tools and requirements, which should be used in a strategic manner, are a critical component in ensuring that the Federal Government maintains a world-class workforce to serve the American people.

Handbook Organization

The Human Resources Flexibilities and Authorities Handbook is divided into three parts.

Part I describes how the Governmentwide HR practices convey the message that the Federal Government is a "single employer" with common policies.

Part II is designed for the non-executive workforce (e.g., General Schedule, Federal Wage System). It will help to:

- Learn what is available to assist in developing integrated and merit-based systems that make sense for the organization

- Foster greater balance of employees' work and nonwork time for greater productivity and higher morale

- Inject new skills and competencies into the workforce

- Develop compensation, performance and reward systems that send clear messages high performance is valued and rewarded

- Tackle workforce challenges in general

Part III is devoted to the flexibilities and authorities designed specifically for the Senior Executive Service.

Retaining and Motivating the Workforce

Many organizational strategies focus primarily on monetary benefits to retain and motivate quality employees. However, pay often is not the most important reason cited by employees for being satisfied with their jobs or wanting to continue to work for a particular organization. When applying the flexibilities and authorities in this handbook, agencies should also assess (including how successfully they were used and how important they turned out to be) the use of non-monetary strategies and factors, such as the following:

- Opportunities for career growth and improvement in skills, including formal training and on-the-job learning and development;

- Mentoring employees to help advance their careers and build their networks;
- Policies and programs that promote diversity and inclusion in the workplace.
- Understanding how work fits in with and contributes to the agency's goals and priorities;
- Performance appraisals that provide timely and constructive feedback and reflect fairly on performance;
- "Open door" policies that help to foster good working relationships and effective team work;
- Alternative work schedules (flexible work hours/days);
- Family-friendly leave options;
- Opportunity to telework;
- Supportive Work/Life and health and wellness policies; and
- Positive, healthy work environment.

Additional Resources

The U.S. Office of Personnel Management (OPM) is the central source for information on Governmentwide regulations, policies, guidance, and human resources tools and flexibilities for Federal HR management.

For the latest information on Federal human resources policies, please visit OPM's website at http://www.opm.gov.

For the latest information on civilian employment opportunities with the Federal Government, see USAJOBS.gov.[1]

For a one-stop resource for effective Federal recruiting in today's digital employment market place, including best practices and accurate and consistent information on recruiting and hiring in the Federal Government, see www.USAJOBSRecruit.gov.

For the latest statistical data on the Federal workforce, see Fedscope at http://www.fedscope.opm.gov/.

---

[1] As discussed below, agencies may not be required to post vacancies for certain positions on USAJOBS. Accordingly, potential applicants may also wish to review the Web sites of particular agencies in which they are interested in working.

This page intentionally left blank.

Table of Contents

This page intentionally left blank.

PART I: GOVERNMENTWIDE INTERESTS

For certain aspects of human resources management, conceiving of the Government as a "single employer" remains sound public policy. Consequently, it is important to retain Governmentwide approaches, authorities, entitlements, and requirements in several areas, including:

- Accountability for adherence to merit system principles
- Employee protection from prohibited personnel practices
- Veterans preference in employment and retention
- A Governmentwide benefits system for retirement, insurance, and leave
- A Governmentwide system for determining annual adjustments to the pay structures for General Schedule, Prevailing Rate System, and other employees
- A statutory collective bargaining framework for labor management relations
- A system of procedural protections for employees related to adverse actions
- A Governmentwide system for collecting and publishing workforce information
- Executive management by members of the Senior Executive Service and its equivalents
- Oversight by OPM

In addition, certain principles that promote the public interest can guide agencies as they make use of the flexibilities described in this document. Such principles include:

- Maintaining budget discipline as human resources systems and authorities are changed
- Making organizational improvements with employees and their representatives in accordance with whatever bargaining and consultation rights are invoked by employee representatives
- Enhancing interagency mobility (i.e., policies that do not inhibit or discourage movement in or out of the agency)
- Avoiding the escalation of payroll costs driven primarily by interagency competition for employees

Within these broad parameters, agencies are free to make immediate use of the existing human resources flexibilities listed in Parts II and III of this document.

This page intentionally left blank.

PART II: EXISTING HUMAN RESOURCES FLEXIBILITIES AND AUTHORITIES

A.   *STAFFING THE ORGANIZATION*

Contact: employ@opm.gov

Federal agencies have many flexibilities and authorities available to hire new employees for permanent and for short and long-term assignments. The following is a list of methods and flexibilities agencies can use immediately to attract and retain quality employees.

1.   USAJOBS and USAJOBSRecruit-Recruiting Tool for Agencies

USAJOBS is the mechanism by which agencies and OPM fulfill their statutory obligations to post information concerning opportunities to participate in examinations for positions in the competitive service and to maintain a comprehensive list of all announcements of vacant positions in the competitive service that are to be filled by appointment for more than one year and for which applications are being or will soon be accepted from outside the hiring agency's workforce. See 5 U.S.C. 3327, 3330. It is also the mechanism by which OPM will announce the opportunity to apply for the Presidential Management Fellows program and apprise potential applicants of positions that agencies intend to fill using the other two Pathways Programs (discussed below). *See* 5 CFR. 362.203(a)(2), 362.303(a)(2), 362.403(a); *see also* 77 F.R. 28194, 28198 (May 11, 2012) ("OPM will make this information available to the public. Our intention is to do so through USAJOBS.gov . . . ."). Finally, USAJOBS may be used by agencies to advertise vacancies, even when posting there is not required (for example, when the position to be filled is in the excepted service and not covered by the Pathways regulations). In that sense, USAJOBS is the Federal Government's centralized one-stop shopping service for agency vacancy announcements and various items of relevant employment information available 24/7. Because agency job postings and employment information can be located in one Governmentwide system, it saves considerable time and resources for both users and Federal agencies. As a testament to its success, the number of job announcements has steadily increased over the last few years to well over 30,000.

USAJOBS is accessible through www.USAJOBS.gov. Vacancy announcements and employment information are available to all agency staff, job seekers, Federal employees, and the general public.

USAJOBS offers a variety of features to support recruiting efforts of Federal agencies:
- A wide array of potential job searches includes: jobs by location, agency, series, and by keywords.
- Employment information fact sheets, including agency-specific fact sheets, discuss a wide variety of topics related to Federal employment issues.
- A capability for job seekers to specify up to ten customized job searches and then receive an automatic email when new jobs are posted that match those search criteria. The emails provide links directly to the vacancy announcements.

- Agency search pages can be created for any agency to advertise either internal or external positions.
- A Hot Jobs area available to agencies for posting of critical or hard-to-fill jobs. This provides essential visibility to job seekers one click from the home page. Agencies should contact USAJOBS@opm.gov to display its jobs in this area.
- Featured Jobs and Featured Employer links in the USAJOBS home page are two additional tools agencies can use to further expose its announcements and agency information. Contact USAJOBS@opm.gov to learn more about these marketing tools.
- Banner ads for an agency with special hiring needs.
- A resume builder feature that allows individuals to create and save up to five resumes. Users can then use these resumes to apply online when they are ready. Job seekers can choose to make their resumes "searchable" and thus increase the likelihood they will be invited to apply for hard-to-fill positions by Federal agencies conducting resume mining.
- USAJOBS.gov/STUDENTJOBS provides a one-stop shopping service designed for student opportunities within the Federal Government. It includes some of the same features as USAJOBS: a job search database, USAJOBS by Email, the resume builder, and employment information fact sheets.

As part of its continuing efforts to modernize and streamline the hiring process, OPM encourages agencies to accept job resumes online. Now that agencies have the capability to use the Internet and make use of automation, they should seek new and improved ways to continue automating hiring processes, e.g., accepting online resumes. Such improvements also provide better service to job seekers.

USAJOBSRecruit is a one-stop gateway to recruitment resources for Federal employees to receive information and collaborate on recruiting in the Federal Government. This website provides HR professionals, hiring managers, recruiters, and all Federal employees with information, resources, and knowledge sharing opportunities in the areas of workforce planning, recruiting strategies, marketing, and effectiveness. Through multi-media learning tools, discussion forums, chats, and blogs, members learn from their peers and experts in the field about how to recruit and retain a Federal world-class workforce. Visit www.USAJOBSRecruit.gov to learn more.

2.   Recruiting and Examining Job Applicants

Agencies generally have the authority to:

- Conduct competitive examining for all positions in the competitive service (except administrative law judges) under delegation agreements between OPM and the agencies. (Pub. L. 104-52; 5 U.S.C. 1104(a)(2); 5 CFR 2.1)

- Use commercial recruiting firms and nonprofit employment services to recruit for vacancies, subject to the provisions of 5 CFR part 300, subpart D.

- Hire by any of the methods authorized in title 5 of the Code of Federal Regulations. (5 CFR 7.1, 330.102)

- Use category rating selection procedures authorized at 5 U.S.C. 3319, as part of the competitive examining process. Under category rating, applicants who meet basic qualification requirements established for the position are evaluated against job-related competencies or knowledge, skills and abilities (KSAs) then ranked by being placed in one of two or more predefined quality categories instead of being ranked in numeric score order. Preference eligibles are placed ahead of non-preference eligibles within each quality category. For positions other than scientific and professional positions at GS-9 equivalent or higher, qualified preference-eligibles with a compensable service-connected disability of 10 percent or more shall be listed in the highest quality category. Veterans' preference is absolute within each quality category. Pursuant to Improving the Federal Recruitment and Hiring Process, a Presidential Memorandum of May 11, 2010, an agency is now generally required to use the category rating approach unless it obtains an exception from the Director of OPM, in consultation with the Office of Management and Budget. Id. at §§ 1(a)(3), 5(d).

3.   Short-term Staffing Options

Agencies have the authority to:

- Bring in temporary assignees from state and local governments, colleges and universities, Indian tribal governments, and eligible not-for-profit organizations under the Intergovernmental Personnel Act (IPA) Mobility Program. Assignments should be made for the mutual benefit of the Federal Government and the non-Federal entity, and are for 2 years. Assignments may be extended for an additional 2 years, allowing for a maximum term of 4 consecutive years. Assignees are either temporarily appointed to the Federal agency or serve while on detail. Cost-sharing arrangements for mobility assignments are negotiated between the participating organizations. The Federal agency may agree to pay all, some, or none of the costs associated with the assignment. Such costs may include basic pay, supplemental pay, benefits, and travel and relocation expenses. (5 U.S.C. 3371-3375; 5 CFR part 334)

- Use temporary appointments for short-term needs not expected to last longer than one year. Recruitment is accomplished through the competitive process. (5 CFR part 316, subpart D)

- Use term appointments for more than one and up to four years in circumstances where the need for the employee's services is not permanent, including but not limited to: project work; extraordinary workload; scheduled abolishment, reorganization, or contracting out of the function; uncertainty of future funding; or the need to maintain permanent positions for placement of employees who would otherwise be displaced from other parts of the organization. Recruitment is accomplished through the competitive process. (5 CFR part 316, subpart C)

- Allow details of their employees within a Department for up to 120 days. Intra-agency details in increments of 120 days are allowed when approved by the head of the Department. (5 U.S.C. 3341)

- Employ experts or consultants for temporary or intermittent employment. The excepted service appointment is used to hire experts and consultants under 5 U.S.C. 3109, to perform temporary (not to exceed one year) or intermittent expert or consultant work. (This differs from employing experts and consultants through procurement contracts, which are covered by regulations issued by the Federal Acquisition Regulation Council.) Under 5 CFR part 304, an expert is someone who is specifically qualified by education and experience to perform difficult and challenging tasks in a particular field beyond the usual range of achievement. A consultant is someone who can provide valuable and pertinent advice generally drawn from a high degree of broad administrative, professional, or technical knowledge or experience. (5 U.S.C. 3109; 5 CFR part 304; agency specific legislation)

- Use commercial temporary help services for brief periods (120 days, with extension of additional 120 days) for short-term situations. This option may be used only when regular recruitment and hiring procedures are impractical, and the commercial service is purchased through the Federal procurement system. (5 CFR part 300, subpart E)

- Choose to enter into various types of contracts, where appropriate. These contracts follow Federal procurement regulations.

4. Alternative Staffing Options

- Pathways for Students and Recent Graduates. Executive Order 13562, December 27, 2010, calls for streamlined pathways into Federal service for students and recent graduates. The Pathways Program regulations took effect on July 10, 2012 (see 77 FR 28194). OPM is working to build a Governmentwide culture that encourages agency leaders to engage these populations. The Pathways Programs consist of:

    - Internship Program. The Internship Program will replace the current Student Temporary Employment Program and Student Career Experience Program. It will target students enrolled in a wide variety of educational institutions from high school to graduate level. It will provide students opportunities to explore Federal careers while being paid for the work performed. The Internship Program will offer agencies the flexibility to hire students on a short-term basis (not to exceed one year) or for longer periods of time necessary for the students to complete their education.

    - Recent Graduates Program. This brand new one-year developmental program will enable agencies to better recruit from recent graduates of trade and vocational schools, community colleges, universities, and other qualifying educational institutions or programs.

    - Presidential Management Fellows Program. For more than three decades, the PMF Program has been the Federal Government's premier leadership development program for advance degree candidates. The Program focuses on developing a cadre of potential Government leaders. Under Pathways, the eligibility window for applicants will be expanded; graduates will have 2 years from completion of degree requirements to apply to the program. Successful applicants will be placed in a 2-year career development program that offers non-competitive conversion to the competitive service at agency discretion.

- Veterans Employment Opportunities Act. The Veterans Employment Opportunities Act (VEOA) of 1998, as amended, provides that agencies must allow eligible veterans to apply for positions announced under merit promotion procedures when the agency is recruiting from outside its own workforce. ("Agency," in this context, means the parent agency, i.e., Treasury, not the Internal Revenue Service.) A VEOA eligible who competes under merit promotion procedures and is selected will be given a career or career-conditional appointment. Veterans' preference is not a factor in these appointments. (5 U.S.C. 3304(f); 5 CFR 315.611; 335.106)

- Veterans Recruitment Appointments. Agencies have the authority to appoint veterans in the excepted service under the Veterans Recruitment Appointment. This is a special authority under which agencies can appoint an eligible veteran up through the GS-11 or equivalent grade level without competition. The candidate must meet specific eligibility requirements along with the applicable qualification requirements. The agency must convert the appointment to career or career-conditional after 2 years of satisfactory service. (5 CFR part 307)

- Non-competitive appointment authority for certain disabled veterans. Agencies may give a non-competitive temporary appointment of more than 60 days or a term appointment to 30 percent or more disabled veterans:
  - Retired from active military service with a disability rating of 30 percent or more; or
  - Rated by the Department of Veterans Affairs (VA) as having a compensable service-connected disability of 30 percent or more.

There is no grade-level limitation for this authority, but the appointee must meet all qualification requirements, including any written test requirement. The agency may convert the employee's appointment, without a break in service, to a career or career-conditional appointment at any time during the employee's temporary or term appointment. (5 U.S.C. 3112; 5 CFR 316.302, 316.402, and 315.707)

- Non-competitive appointment authority for certain military spouses. This authority allows agencies to appoint a military spouse without competition. Agencies can choose to use this authority when filling competitive service positions on a temporary (not to exceed 1 year), term (more than 1 year but not more than 4 years), or permanent basis. The authority does not entitle spouses to an appointment over any other applicant. Eligible military spouses are those whose active duty military spouse: 1) receives a Permanent Change of Station (PCS) move; 2) has a 100 percent disability rating; or 3) died while on active duty. (5 CFR 315.612)

- Direct-Hire. This authority allows agencies with delegated examining authority to hire individuals without regard to sections 3309-3318 of title 5, United States Code, to positions for which:
  - o Public notice has been given, *and*
  - o The U.S. Office of Personnel Management determines there is a *severe shortage* of candidates or a *critical hiring* need.

OPM may issue direct-hire authority for one or more of the following: occupational series, grades (or equivalent), and geographical location. Requests for direct-hire authority must be submitted by the agency's Chief Human Capital Officer (or equivalent) at the agency's headquarters level (5 CFR 337.201). Agency requests may be addressed to the Associate Director for Employee Services. Agencies can expedite OPM processing by faxing the request to Employee Services at 202-606-2329.

For information on direct hire authorities, including a list of Governmentwide direct-hire authorities, please visit http://www.opm.gov/policy-data-oversight/hiring-authorities/competitive-hiring/#url=Types-of-Appointments. (5 U.S.C. 3304 and 5 CFR part 337, subpart B)

- Special Appointing Authorities: Excepted Service, Schedule A and Schedule B (5 CFR part 213).
  - o Governmentwide schedules A and B: The President or OPM may except positions from the competitive service when the President or OPM determines use of the competitive examination process is not practicable when filling the positions. For example, Attorney positions are excepted from the competitive service and placed under schedule A because OPM is precluded from examining for attorney positions. Similarly, when a specific vacancy is filled through the authority for the appointment of persons with intellectual disabilities, severe physical disabilities, or psychiatric disabilities, the position moves to the excepted service because it is deemed to be impracticable to examine the individuals covered by this authority. The President or OPM may also except positions from the competitive service for which it is not practicable to hold a competitive examination. For example, agencies sometimes have need for special executive department positions established in connection with Senior Executive Service candidate development programs.

  - o Agency specific schedules A and B: OPM may grant agencies specific excepted appointing authorities after considering occupation and duties, reasons why attempts to hold competition are not effective, and reasons why recruitment and competitive examining are not possible, and after reviewing remedies and alternatives that have been used to resolve recruitment and examining problems.

- Job Sharing and Other Permanent Positions That Are Not Full-time. Making appointments with varying work schedules such as part-time (which may include job-sharing arrangements), intermittent, and seasonal is a viable option to manage fluctuating and less than full-time workforce needs. Intermittent work schedules are used only when the nature of the work is sporadic and unpredictable. Seasonal work involves annually recurring periods of work that are expected to last at least 6 months during a calendar year. The use of varying work schedules may attract applicants who prefer to work less than full time. (See Section C for other Work Arrangements & Work/Life Policies that promote a more flexible workforce.) (5 CFR part 340)

- Re-employing annuitants without salary offset. Generally, non-disability annuitants who are reemployed continue to receive their annuity, but their salary is offset by the amount of their annuity (prorated if re-employment is part-time), and they can earn additional annuity rights with substantial service (1 year or more). Under certain limited circumstances, however, the retirement law permits an agency to request that OPM grant a waiver of this offset to help the agency meet certain exceptional employment needs. 5 U.S.C. 8344(i) and 8468(f); 5 CFR part 553. Waivers may be granted on a case-by-case basis, for example, for employees in positions for which there is exceptional difficulty in recruiting or retaining a qualified employee, or for necessary temporary employment due to an emergency involving a direct threat to life or property, or other unusual circumstances. Within the Executive Branch, authority to grant these waivers, or delegate such authority to an agency head, generally rests with OPM. When an annuitant is employed with a waiver, he or she receives full annuity and salary. No additional annuity benefits can be based upon service performed under a waiver, and no retirement deductions are taken. Such employment is subject to Social Security deductions. (5 CFR part 553)

A similar authority permits the heads of agencies to approve waivers under limited circumstances specified in a separate statutory provision, without OPM approval. The authority for this provision is set forth in set forth in 5 U.S.C. 8344(l) and 8468(i).

5.   Probationary Period

With certain exceptions, agencies have the discretion to remove new appointees, supervisors, and managers during their probationary period with few procedural requirements. (5 CFR part 315, subparts H and I)

6.   Workforce Restructuring

Contact: employ@opm.gov

Management Considerations:

"Restructuring" includes organizational decisions that result in actions such as reshaping, downsizing, realigning, reorganizing, streamlining, etc. A restructuring plan helps agency managers develop substantive organizational goals based on fiscal constraints, decisions made by higher level agency managers, decisions made by managers elsewhere in the executive branch (e.g., Office of Management and Budget), legislative action, or judicial or other appellate action.

In developing its restructuring plan the agency should concurrently identify key personnel-related issues that affect the agency's present and future ability to perform its missions, including:

- Excess positions due to the reorganized, reduced, or redirected mission.
- Positions still needed to perform the agency's work.
- Available mechanisms that may help an agency to avoid a reduction in force *(if the agency so chooses)* if the restructuring plan results in excess positions.
- Whether the human resources organization requires additional resources to implement the planned organizational change (e.g., whether agency personnel records and human resources staff are ready to support restructuring actions; or if not ready, how many full time equivalents are needed for what period of time).

In planning for restructuring actions, management should consider:

- Scope - What is the size of the downsizing/restructuring? Is it driven by budget, program shifts, skill imbalances, or mandatory legislative or agency employment reductions? The size, type, and the time available affect the decision about which tools are best for the situation.

- Timing - The more time available, the better, and the less likely the need for drastic measures such as reduction in force. An agency should start as soon as possible by identifying where cuts must be made and concentrating tools and strategies there.

- Targeting - Targeted cuts are more effective than across-the-board cuts, which can leave the agency without the staff to perform critical functions. An agency should identify which functions to end, consolidate, and keep and subsequently identify and target the affected positions.

- Flexibility - There are multiple strategies available for downsizing or restructuring. An agency should be flexible. Strategies should be compatible with the agency's mission and goals.

Multiple Strategies: The following tools and strategies are available to downsize and restructure. Management should consider the alternatives that best fit the situation.

- Intra-Agency Selection Priority Program - A strong internal placement program with selection priority can actively place surplus employees into continuing vacant positions within the agency. Consideration should also be given to related alternatives such as a general freeze on filling vacant positions from both internal and external sources, and offering voluntary early retirement and/or buyouts to increase the number of vacancies available for the placement of surplus and displaced employees.

- Freeze Hiring and Promotions - This can reduce personnel costs. Management should structure a freeze on personnel actions to best fit the agency's individual situation rather than automatically adopting a blanket freeze on all personnel actions. An immediate result of a freeze on filling new positions is a relative stabilization of personnel costs. When combined with expected continuing attrition from the agency, a freeze on filling new positions can actually reduce personnel costs, particularly over a longer period of time. On the down side, a freeze on filling new positions may eventually restrict the capacity of the agency to perform its work, especially if continuing attrition reduces the number of available employees below a critical level.

Agencies can limit hiring more easily than promotions. For example, a "1 for 2" or similar limit on replacement hiring is often more effective than a total freeze. Promotion freezes are more difficult to administer. When effecting freezes, the following should be considered:

- o Will the freeze affect all promotions, only promotions for certain positions, or only promotions at certain grade levels?
- o Will career ladder promotions or promotions based on accretion of duties continue?
- o How will freezing promotions affect morale?
- o Will there be a "safety valve" policy permitting exceptions to the freeze?

- Voluntary Reduction of Hours - Employees may be willing to reduce their hours or convert to a part-time work schedule to avoid more drastic cost-cutting measures. Employees may view such a reduction as an opportunity to meet family or educational needs. An employee survey can be used to determine the interest level and project cost savings (e.g., What grade levels? How many hours?).

A reduction in an employee's scheduled work time will result in an immediate reduction in personnel costs, but will result in a loss of organizational productivity. However, the agency should advise employees of the personal implications of the reduction in hours. For example, an employee who converts from a permanent full-time to a permanent part-time schedule follows a different formula to calculate health benefits costs. Similarly, an employee on voluntary or involuntary leave-without-pay may have a reduction in the leave or retirement credit the employee would have earned had the employee been in a full-time pay and duty status.

- Voluntary Leave Without Pay - Employees may be willing to take 1 day of leave without pay in each pay period, for example, to reduce personnel costs. An employee survey can be used to determine the interest level and project cost savings.

NOTE: Agencies considering voluntary reduction of hours or voluntary leave without pay must make every effort to avoid the appearance of coercion. These are voluntary actions employees can take to help the agency lessen the impact of a budget reduction. Placing an employee on leave without pay without his or her clear consent is an adverse action. Involuntary reduction in the hours of an employee may, in many cases, require the application of reduction in force (RIF) procedures.

- Voluntary Change to Lower Grade - An agency can offer an employee a voluntary change to lower grade without using RIF procedures. In some situations, a voluntary change to lower grade allows an agency to staff a vacancy with a proven employee, while providing continued employment to a surplus employee without forcing RIF actions.

Employees have the right to RIF competition and protections before they are involuntarily downgraded due to reorganization, lack of work, shortage of funds, or insufficient personnel ceiling. An agency may offer grade or pay retention to employees accepting a voluntary change to lower grade under certain conditions. (5 CFR parts 351 and 536)

- Separate Temporary Employees - Competitive service temporary employees, and most excepted service temporary employees, can be terminated without regard to OPM's RIF regulations. (5 CFR 351.501(b), 351.502(b)) The termination of a temporary employee may provide the agency with additional fiscal resources and/or a position to place a surplus or displaced employee.

- Separate Reemployed Annuitants – A reemployed annuitant serves at the will of the agency and, regardless of type of appointment, can be terminated without regard to OPM's RIF regulations. Releasing a reemployed annuitant may also save payroll dollars and free up a position to place a permanent surplus or excess employee. (5 U.S.C. 3323(b)(1))

- Furloughs - An agency may reduce personnel costs by furloughing employees for short periods. Furloughs of 30 continuous days or less, or 22 discontinuous workdays or less, are implemented through adverse action procedures. (5 CFR 351.203, 752.401(a)(5) This means an agency must notify employees 30 days in advance. Employees may appeal a furlough action to the Merit Systems Protection Board.

  Furloughs of more than 30 continuous calendar days, or more than 22 discontinuous workdays, are implemented through RIF procedures. (5 CFR 351.203) This means an agency must notify employees 60 days in advance. As noted above, employees may appeal a furlough action to the Merit Systems Protection Board.

  Furlough is not an option if the agency finds it is faced with a continuing rather than temporary lack of work and/or funds. For example, an agency may furlough an employee (under RIF regulations) only when the agency plans to recall the employee to duty in the position the employee held when furloughed within 1 year. (5 CFR 351.604(a).)

- Details - An agency can detail employees in 120-day increments to other positions within the agency to fill a temporary need.

  An agency can also detail employees to other organizations in the same or a different agency on a reimbursable basis. This works well when other agencies need the specific skills of the employees in the first agency. This may not be viable for agencies downsizing or restructuring.

  NOTE: Competitive procedures are required to detail an employee to a higher-graded position for more than 120 days. (5 CFR part 335)

- Reassign Employees - An agency may reassign an employee to another position at the same grade, either within a local commuting area or to another commuting area. (5 CFR 335.102) The agency must have a legitimate management need for the reassignment and the employee must qualify. An agency may reassign employees in surplus positions into vacant continuing positions in unaffected organizations. Unless an agency has a policy or collective bargaining agreement addressing management's right to reassign in a particular context, it can reassign an employee without regard to his or her relative RIF retention standing. In other words, the agency need not consider veterans' preference, length of service, or performance ratings in reassigning employees.

  Reassignment to a position in a different local commuting area does not provide the right to compete for a position in the present competitive area under 5 CFR part 351 RIF regulations even if the employee declines the reassignment and the agency subsequently separates the employee under 5 CFR part 752 adverse action regulations.

- The RIF regulations need not be followed if the employee is reassigned to a position at the same grade, and if the reassignment does not require displacement. (5 CFR 351.201(a)(2)) The agency must follow RIF procedures if involuntarily separating or downgrading the employee as part of a reorganization.

- Voluntary Relocation - Employees may be willing to voluntarily relocate outside the local commuting area. Agencies should consider cost of travel and relocation expenses, cost-of-living expenses, and grade-level differences between offices, and any necessary orientation or retraining costs required.

- Train Employees for Other Positions - An agency may train (or retrain) employees for placement into continuing vacant positions as another alternative to minimize involuntary separations and demotions by reduction in force. An effective intra-agency training and retraining program allows an agency to retain its valuable employees even if they currently hold surplus positions.

  Academic degree training. Section 4107 of 5 U.S.C., provides an agency with additional opportunities for training employees when this training is needed to resolve a staffing problem identified by the agency (e.g., a shortage of employees with specific skills) to meet an identified agency training need, or to accomplish the goals of the agency's restructuring plan.

- Train Employees for Positions in Other Agencies - 5 U.S.C. 4103(b) allows an agency to train surplus employees to help place them in other agencies. The statute requires the agency head to determine the training is in the Government's interest. The agency head must consider several factors in selecting an employee for training, including use of the employee's current skills, knowledge, and abilities in the new position; the employee's capability to learn skills and acquire the knowledge and abilities needed; and potential benefits to the Government resulting from training.

Note: An agency may use its appropriated funds for training or retraining surplus or displaced employees for positions outside the Federal Government only when specifically authorized by legislation. (5 CFR 410.308(c)(3)

- Intra-Agency Career Transition Assistance Programs - If an agency finds implementation of its restructuring plan will likely result in involuntary separations, demotions, and/or relocations because some employees hold surplus positions, the agency's first option is often to try to place the surplus employees in other continuing positions through an effective outplacement program. Career Transition Assistance Plans (CTAP) provide most surplus and displaced permanent competitive service employees with intra-agency selection priority for vacancies the agency is filling in the current local commuting area. CTAP also requires the agency to provide specific career transition services, such as:

  o Career counseling
  o Career transition services and facilities (which may be onsite or at a different location)
  o Application referrals
  o Job search counseling
  o An orientation session for surplus and displaced employees that explains both how to use the agency's career transition services, and what the eligibility requirements are for selection priority under available programs

  5 CFR part 330, subpart F, of OPM's regulations covers CTAP.

- Interagency Career Transition Assistance Program - Interagency Career Transition Assistance Plans (ICTAP) provide most displaced permanent competitive service employees with selection priority over other outside candidates who apply for vacancies that other agencies are filling in the employee's current local commuting area.

  5 CFR part 330, subpart G, of OPM's regulations covers ICTAP.

- Voluntary Early Retirement Authority (VERA or "early out"). The VERA option allows permanent employees to retire early if their organization is undergoing a substantial RIF, a substantial reorganization, a substantial transfer of function, or other substantial workforce restructuring and reshaping. VERA is a valuable tool to increase voluntary attrition to create placement opportunities for employees who would otherwise be involuntarily separated or downgraded, and to avoid displacements in actual RIF competition. The agency should consider other alternatives that would also minimize the need for RIF (e.g., furlough, career transition assistance programs, or hiring freezes) before requesting VERA from OPM. An agency should not use VERA as a quick fix for a short-term immediate problem (e.g., to achieve short-term budgetary savings for the remainder of a fiscal year or to temporarily reduce a ceiling).

  An agency may offer VERA to its employees consistent with its authorization from OPM. To be eligible for VERA, a non-temporary employee must be age 50 with 20 years of creditable service, or have 25 years of creditable service at any age (see 5 CFR 831.114 and 5 CFR 842.213).

The agency may make VERA offers based on skills, knowledge, and other position factors, as well as classification series, occupations, organization, etc. For additional information on VERA and/or to submit a request to OPM, the agency should contact employ@opm.gov.

- Voluntary Separation Incentive Payments (VSIP, or "buyouts") - The VSIP option allows an agency in a restructuring situation to offer to a permanent employee a lump-sum payment up to $25,000 if the employee voluntarily retires or resigns. Chapter 35 of title 5, U.S. Code provides a buyout authority to most executive branch agencies that are carrying out restructuring actions. The maximum amount of a buyout is capped at $25,000; however, each agency head may now determine the maximum amount of a buyout up to the $25,000 ceiling.

  Each agency wishing to offer buyouts under chapter 35 must submit a plan to OPM that identifies the purpose, coverage, time periods, and amounts of the proposed buyouts. OPM will consult with OMB in reviewing the agency's buyout plan. OPM will subsequently notify the agency in writing when the buyout plan is approved. For additional information on VSIP and/or to submit a request to OPM, the agency should contact employ@opm.gov and consult the applicable regulations at 5 CFR part 576.

- Discontinued Service Retirement (DSR) - An employee may be eligible for an immediate DSR annuity if the employee is separated involuntarily, except by removal for cause for misconduct or delinquency. An employee is not eligible for DSR if the agency offers another position in the same commuting area within two grades of the employee's current position that has the same tenure and work schedule and for which the employee is qualified. An employee must be age 50 with 20 years of creditable service, or have 25 years of creditable service at any age to be eligible for DSR. (5 CFR 831.503, 842.206)

- Workforce Investment Act of 1998 (WIA) - The WIA provides both training and retraining options to assist displaced employees unlikely to return to their previous occupation. The WIA program is administered by the Department of Labor. The WIA provides a wide range of services to help individuals displaced from their positions because of restructuring. These services include skills assessments, job development, counseling, job search assistance, and training or retraining. Specific services are available through state and local employment offices. The Department of Labor's web site provides links to States' WIA offices and other state and local services for displaced employees at http://www.doleta.gov/usworkforce/onestop/onestopmap.cfm

7.   Other Resources

There are other online hiring resources available. The OPM Federal Hiring Flexibilities Resource Center at http://www.opm.gov/Strategic_Management_of_Human_Capital/fhfrc/default.asp has more in-depth information on:

- Appointing Veterans
- Direct-Hire Authority

- Student Employment
- Excepted Service
- Category Rating

More resources and links are on the OPM Hiring Toolkit site at http://www.opm.gov/policy-data-oversight/human-capital-management/hiring-reform/.

B.   *STRATEGIC HUMAN CAPITAL MANAGEMENT*

The Strategic Management of Human Capital is a critical component that lends to the effective and efficient operation of Government. Strategic Human Capital Management (SHCM) is intended to help Federal agency leaders better manage their organizations' most important asset—their people. Federal agencies that acquire, develop, and retain high-performing employees with the appropriate skills and competencies are better able to respond to the needs of the public on a daily basis and in times of crisis.

The role of the Government is continuously evolving; therefore, the roles of Federal agencies and thus Federal employees continue to change. This has added to the current workforce challenges of needing to fill the gaps that will be left by the increasing number of retiring "baby boomer" leaders, the need to attract new talent with cutting edge skills and competencies,; and the need to revamp performance management systems—all on increasingly tight budgets. Consequently, the need for SHCM, with its emphasis on achieving results, continues to serve a key role for human resources management (HRM) practices in the Government.

The management of human capital needs to be efficient and effective to make the Federal Government competitive for the best talent America has to offer. In order to effectively manage workforce challenges, agencies are strongly encouraged to utilize the principles of the Human Capital Assessment and Accountability Framework (HCAAF), in conjunction with the principles of the End-to-End (E-2-E) hiring model, to transform their workforce.

1.   Human Capital Assessment and Accountability Framework (HCAAF)

Establishment of the HCAAF, and its related standards and metrics, fulfilled OPM's mandate under the CHCO Act, as codified at 5 U.S.C. 1103(c), to design systems and set standards, including appropriate metrics, for assessing the management of human capital by Federal agencies. The HCAAF consolidates and augments earlier guidance and is structured to help agencies determine what they need to do, how they can do it, and how they can measure human capital program and initiative success. It also fuses human capital management to merit system principles—a cornerstone of the United States Civil Service—and other Civil Service laws, rules, and regulations.

The HCAAF consists of five human capital systems which together provide a consistent, comprehensive representation of effective and efficient human capital management for the Federal Government. The HCAAF systems include:

- Strategic Alignment (Planning and Goal Setting)
- Leadership and Knowledge Management (Implementation)
- Results-Oriented Performance Culture (Implementation)
- Talent Management (Implementation)
- Accountability (Evaluating Results)

The HCAAF can be found in its entirety with definitions of the systems, standards and metrics at http://www.opm.gov/hcaaf_resource_center/. See also HCAAF Systems, Standards, and Metrics.

2.   The OPM Workforce Planning Model

Through workforce planning, agencies are able to identify work activities and required competencies to support agency mission as part of developing model organizations. Workforce planning helps agencies to specify the type and number of employees needed to effectively carry out mission-critical work.

A sound workforce planning methodology includes the development of practical workforce strategies to include recruiting, retention and shaping. These strategies require the support and participation of executive leadership, management, employees, and agency staff responsible for financial management, acquisition, and human resources. A good workforce planning process includes a comprehensive communication plan and change management mechanisms to allow agency personnel to adjust recruiting and retention strategies due to possible changes in mission and/or resourcing.

The OPM Workforce Planning Model provides a six-step (step 6 is an extension of the process evaluation and monitoring step) approach to developing a successful workforce plan that provides managers with a framework for making human resource decisions based on the organization's mission, strategic plan, budgetary resources, and set of desired workforce competencies. The model can also link human resource initiatives that sometimes seem disconnected from other facets of the management strategy.

Workforce planning is an essential component of how organizations are able to strategically manage their human capital. It is a comprehensive and on-going process that does not occur in isolation as each step of the strategic management of human capital is dependent upon the others.

The six-steps of OPM's workforce model (including the extended 6th-step) are:

Step 1- Set Strategic Direction: Enables agencies to align the workforce planning process with the agency's strategic plan, annual performance and business plans and work activities. This includes identifying the organizational direction while ensuring that all supporting plans and documentation link to the workforce planning efforts. Also, agencies should review the organizational structure to assess whether its current structure will be able to achieve the mission and goals of the agency. This is also the step where organizations may want to consider Business Process Reengineering to optimize internal processes.

Step 1 of the workforce planning process is an optimal time to solicit support of stakeholders (e.g., executive leadership, information technology, budget/finance, human resources and hiring managers) so that roles and responsibilities for the process can be established. In addition, this is the ideal time for human resources to position itself as a strategic partner with other key entities within the organization.

Step 2 - Analyze Workforce (Supply & Demand), Identify Skill Gaps and Conduct Workforce Analysis: Provides approaches that move beyond a "headcount" analysis to an examination of the competencies the workforce will need to be successful. This step also helps agencies quantify the gaps that exist between needs and (current) available resources.

A valuable analytic tool is FedScope, OPM's user-friendly, Internet-based interface to centralized personnel data. It can be accessed at: www.fedscope.opm.gov.

Step 3 - Develop Competency Action Plan: Guides HR Directors and agency managers as they craft actions (e.g., re-training) that focus not only on the current workforce, but also on other potential sources of staff (e.g., new hires, contractors, and a contingent workforce) competencies and the HR infrastructure that need to be in place to support the plan.

Step 4 - Implement Action Plan: Agencies should begin implementing identified actions that are required to insure that goals within each phase of the process are accomplished. In addition, actions should be identified for how recruitment, developmental and retention strategies will be used to support an agency in selecting and/or developing a high quality workforce that will enable an organization to meet its mission.

This is an ideal time to establish a communications and change management plan that will serve as a focal point of communication for employees about the changes brought about during the workforce planning process.

Step 5 - Monitor, Evaluate, Maintain, and Reconcile (Continuous): Assists HR Directors and agency managers in reviewing successes and failures and using that information to modify the workforce plan to address any new workforce and organizational challenges.

Observe, review, and monitor program activities and (internal and external) developments that may affect the action plan, particularly to monitor progress against milestones and measures.

Step 6 - Adjust Plan as needed: As with any project, changes are destined to occur; therefore, adjust the plan as needed to address new workforce issues resulting from changes in mission priorities or resources. It is essential to allocate time and resources to address any modifications that need to be made as a result of any issues that were brought to light during the monitoring and evaluation process.

Agencies can view information about the workforce planning model at: OPM's Workforce Planning Model.

3.   Learning Management Systems/Training Data Systems

Executives and managers must have a comprehensive understanding of the current skills of their staffs, as well as the skills they will need in the future, and include that information in their short and long-term planning. Agencies need to be able to determine what training programs are needed to accomplish their workforce development goals. They need information to substantiate that their expenditures on training have met the intended purpose. There is a demand for evidence to ensure human capital development decisions support the organization's mission and goals. Such evidence can be critical to continued funding. Therefore, it is imperative that comprehensive, accurate, and current training information is available to decision-makers.

In addition to meeting the internal needs of the organization and providing the business case for HRD professionals, collecting training data is essential for meeting certain regulatory requirements. Further, there is a continued emphasis across Government and in Congress for data to support strategic planning, explain expenditures, and justify requests for additional funds (performance-based budgeting). In addition, Federal Government initiatives require agencies to identify long-term strategic goals and describe how the agency intends to achieve those goals through its activities and through its human capital, financial, information, and other resources. This illustrates the importance of effective information management systems which not only maintain training data, but which incorporate data from multiple systems to provide a comprehensive analysis of the agency's performance.

The following publications are useful in developing human capital strategic plans and measuring results:

- A Guide to Strategically Planning Training and Measuring Results
- Training Needs Assessment Handbook
- Training Policy Handbook
- The Guide for Collection and Management of Training Information
- The Training Evaluation Field Guide

These publications are online on the OPM Training Policy website, the OPM Training and Development Wiki or by request via hrdleadership@opm.gov.

4.   Gov Online Learning Center

More information is available at: http://www.hru.gov

HR University is the Federal Government's "one-stop" Human Resources Career Development Center. HRU is aimed at professionalizing the Federal HR career field and is designed to address competency and skill gaps within the HR community, achieve Government-wide savings, identify and offer the best HR training across Government, and establish a means for sharing resources across all agencies.

OPM's Training and Development Wiki's "Sharing Resources and Collaborating Across Agencies" page, created by the Federal Chief Learning Officers Council, in partnership with OPM, is a place where agencies may share resources, materials, and courses, including Federal mandatory training. Materials on this page are free and available for download.

C.   WORK ARRANGEMENTS & WORK/LIFE POLICIES

The Federal Government is a leader in providing family-oriented leave policies and other programs and workplace flexibilities that support a positive, productive work culture and environment. This includes the use of flexible work schedules and telework; leave programs (leave sharing, leave banks, and leave for medical conditions and family responsibilities); part-time employment and job sharing; the Employee Assistance Program; worksite health promotion programs; the Child Care Subsidy Program; on-site child development centers; and information and referral services for child and elder care resources. The Government is committed to supporting employees' ability to effectively manage their work and personal responsibilities.

1.   Hours of Work and Scheduling Flexibilities

Additional information on work schedules is available at: http://www.opm.gov/policy-data-oversight/pay-leave/work-schedules/.

Agencies have the discretionary authority to determine the hours of work for their employees to ensure agencies meet organizational goals and to help employees balance personal needs. (5 U.S.C. chapter 61, subchapters I and II; 5 CFR part 610)

Agencies may establish:

- Full-time, part-time, intermittent, and seasonal work schedules.

- Traditional day shifts, night and weekend duty, rotating shifts, and "first-40" schedules.

- Paid and unpaid breaks in the workday. Additional information on establishing breaks can be obtained at http://www.opm.gov/policy-data-oversight/pay-leave/work-schedules/fact-sheets/lunch-or-other-meal-periods/.

- Alternative work schedules, which can replace traditional schedules (i.e., 8 hours per day/40 hours per week, with fixed starting and stopping times). The Handbook on Alternative Work Schedules provides a framework for Federal agencies to consult in establishing alternative work schedules and provides information to assist agencies in administering such programs. This handbook is on OPM's website at http://www.opm.gov/policy-data-oversight/pay-leave/reference-materials/handbooks/alternative-work-schedules/. Also, information concerning negotiating alternative work schedules can be found in OPM's Labor-Management Relations Guidance Bulletin "Negotiating Flexible and Compressed Work Schedules" at http://www.opm.gov/policy-data-oversight/labor-management-relations/law-policy-resources/#url=Negotiating-Flexible-and-Compressed-Work-Schedules.

Alternative work schedules include:

- Flexible work schedules (FWS) – Within limits set by their agencies, FWS can enable employees to select and alter their work schedules to better fit personal needs and help balance work, personal, and family responsibilities. FWS consist of workdays composed of core hours and flexible hours. Core hours are the designated period of the day when all employees must be at work. Flexible hours are the part of the workday when employees may (within limits or "bands") choose their time of arrival and departure. Certain FWS allow an employee to complete the basic 80-hour biweekly work requirement in less than 10 workdays because of the absence of core hours on one of the normal workdays (e.g., Flexible 5/4-9"). The authority for FWS is contained in 5 U.S.C. 6122.

  An agency's FWS plan may permit employees to earn credit hours. An employee may elect to earn credit hours for working hours in excess of the employee's basic work requirement (e.g., 40 hours a week). An employee may use earned credit hours to take time off and vary the length of a workweek or a workday. Refer to the Handbook on Alternative Work Schedules for more information on the administration of credit hours.

- Compressed work schedules (CWS) - CWS are fixed work schedules that enable full-time employees to complete the basic 80-hour biweekly work requirement in less than 10 workdays. These schedules are authorized by 5 U.S.C. 6127.

  Agencies may adopt either flexible or compressed work schedules for their employees. An employee may not be permitted to work on a "hybrid" schedule that combines aspects of both programs.

- Adjusted work schedules for religious observances are available for employees whose personal religious beliefs require abstaining from work at certain times of the workday or workweek. Modifications in work schedules must not interfere with the efficient accomplishment of an agency's mission. The hours worked in lieu of the normal work schedule do not create any entitlement to premium pay (including overtime pay). Additional information on the adjustment of work schedules for religious observances may be obtained from http://www.opm.gov/policy-data-oversight/pay-leave/work-schedules/fact-sheets/adjustment-of-work-schedules-for-religious-observances/. (5 U.S.C. 5550a; 5 CFR part 550, subpart J)

2. Telework

Contact: Work/Life and Performance Culture Staff at worklife@opm.gov

The official definition of telework can be found in the Telework Enhancement Act of 2010. "The term 'telework' or 'teleworking' refers to a work flexibility arrangement under which an employee performs the duties and responsibilities of such employee's position, and other authorized activities, from an approved worksite other than the location from which the employee would otherwise work." Telework is a work arrangement that allows an employee to perform work, during any part of regular, paid hours, at an approved alternative worksite.

For detailed guidance on telework, please consult our comprehensive central website, www.telework.gov, co-sponsored by OPM and the General Services Administration. A good place to begin is to review the publication *Guide to Telework in the Federal Government*, found in the section "Guidance and Legislation."

3.   Leave

Additional information on Federal leave programs is available at: http://www.opm.gov/policy-data-oversight/pay-leave/leave-administration/

- Annual leave - The annual leave program provides most employees a total of 13, 20, or 26 days of annual leave, depending on years of service. (Most Federal employees may carry a maximum of 240 hours over to the next leave year. Employees stationed outside of the United States may carry over 360 hours. SES, SL, and ST employees may carry over 720 hours.) An employee may use annual leave for vacations, rest and relaxation, and personal business or emergencies. An employee has a right to take annual leave, subject to the right of the supervisor to schedule the time at which annual leave may be taken. (5 U.S.C. chapter 63, subchapter I; 5 CFR part 630, subparts B and C)

- Sick leave programs for family care and bereavement - The sick leave program provides most employees a total of 13 days of sick leave each year (which accumulates without limit in succeeding years). Most Federal employees may use a total of up to 104 hours (13 workdays) of sick leave each leave year to care for a family member who is incapacitated by illness or injury, accompany family members to routine health care appointments, or arrange for or attend the funeral of a family member. An employee may also use a total of up to 12 administrative workweeks of sick leave each leave year to care for a family member with a serious health condition. However, if an employee previously has used any portion of the 13 days of sick leave for general family care or bereavement purposes in a leave year, that amount must be subtracted from the 12-week entitlement. In addition, an employee may use sick leave for absences related to adopting a child. (5 U.S.C. chapter 63, subchapter I; 5 CFR part 630, subparts B and D)

- Advanced Annual and Sick Leave - Advanced annual and sick leave are provided at the discretion of the agency—they are not an employee entitlement. Agencies may grant advanced annual and sick leave consistent with agency policy. The amount of annual leave that may be advanced may not exceed the amount the employee will accrue in the remainder of the leave year. Sick leave may be advanced for all purposes for which sick leave may be granted. The amount of sick leave that may be granted for specific purposes is outlined in the sick leave regulations, with a maximum of 104 hours being advanced for some purposes, and a maximum of 240 hours for others. Two hundred forty hours is the maximum amount of advanced sick leave an employee may have to his or her credit at any one time. (5 U.S.C. chapter 63, subchapter I; 5 CFR part 630, subparts B,C, and D)

- Leave sharing programs allow an employee who has a personal or family medical emergency and who has exhausted his or her own available paid leave (i.e., accrued, accumulated, re-credited, or restored annual and sick leave) to receive donated annual leave from other Federal employees through the voluntary leave transfer or leave bank programs. (5 U.S.C. 6331-6340 and 6361-6373; 5 CFR part 630, subparts I and J)

- Emergency leave transfer program - In the event of a major disaster or emergency as declared by the President, such as floods, earthquakes, tornadoes, or terrorist incidents that result in severe adverse effects for a substantial number of employees, the President may direct OPM to establish an emergency leave transfer program. Under the emergency leave transfer program, an employee or an agency leave bank may donate annual leave for transfer to employees who are adversely affected, or have family members who are adversely affected, by the disaster or emergency. A leave recipient is not required to exhaust all available paid leave prior to receiving and using donated annual leave under the emergency leave transfer program. (5 U.S.C. 6391, 5 CFR part 630, subpart K)

- Under the Family and Medical Leave (FMLA), an employee is entitled to up to 12 administrative workweeks of unpaid leave during any 12-month period for (1) the birth of a child and care of the newborn; (2) the placement of a child with the employee for adoption or foster care; (3) the care of an employee's spouse, child, or parent with a serious health condition; (4) an employee's own serious health condition that makes him or her unable to perform the duties of his or her position; or (5) any qualifying exigency arising out of the fact that the employee's spouse, son, daughter, or parent is a covered military member on covered active duty (or has been notified of an impending call or order to covered active duty) in the Armed Forces. An employee is also entitled to up to 26 workweeks of unpaid leave during any 12-month period to care for a covered service member with a serious injury or illness, incurred or aggravated in the line of duty while on active duty in the Armed Forces, if the employee is the spouse, son, daughter, parent, or next of kin of a covered service member. While using family and medical leave, employees may substitute annual leave or sick leave, as appropriate, for unpaid leave. (5 U.S.C. 6381-6387; 5 CFR part 630, subpart L)

- Leave for bone-marrow and organ donation allows Federal employees to use up to 7 days of paid leave each year (in addition to sick or annual leave) to serve as a bone-marrow donor and up to 30 days of paid leave each year to serve as an organ donor. (5 U.S.C. 6327)

- Time off for volunteer activities – Federal agencies can support employees' commitment to community service by ensuring all employees are aware of the various flexibilities available to them to participate in volunteer activities. Agencies may permit employees to make maximum use of existing flexibilities such as alternative work schedules, annual leave, leave without pay, credit hours under flexible work schedules, compensatory time off, and excused absence (administrative leave), where appropriate, to perform community service. The granting of excused absence for volunteer activities should be limited to those situations in which the employee's absence, in the department's or agency's determination, is not specifically prohibited by law and satisfies one or more of the following criteria: (1) the absence is directly related to the department or agency's mission; (2) the absence is officially sponsored or sanctioned by the head of the department or agency; (3) the absence will clearly enhance the professional development or skills of the employee in his or her current position; or (4) the absence is brief and is determined to be in the interest of the agency. Additional information may be obtained at http://www.opm.gov/policy-data-oversight/pay-leave/leave-administration/fact-sheets/related-information/.

- Enhanced annual leave accrual rates for Senior Executive Service (SES), senior-level (SL) and scientific or professional (ST), and positions in a pay system equivalent to the SES or SL/ST pay system – Members of the SES and employees in SL and ST positions are entitled to accrue annual leave at the rate of 1 day (8 hours) for each full biweekly pay period without regard to the length of their service with the Federal Government. In addition, OPM is authorized to extend the coverage of this provision to employees covered by a pay system determined by OPM to be equivalent to either the SES pay system or the SL/ST pay system. (5 U.S.C. chapter 6303(f), 5 CFR part 630.301)

- Creditable service for annual leave accrual for non-Federal work experience and experience in the Uniformed Service– An employee who is covered by the Federal annual and sick leave program established under chapter 63 of title 5, United States Code, may receive service credit for prior non-Federal work experience or experience in a uniformed service that otherwise would not be creditable for the purpose of determining his or her annual leave accrual rate. An employee may receive credit if the head of the agency determines the employee's experience was obtained in a position having duties directly related to the duties of the position to which the employee is being appointed and the employee's skills and experience are necessary to achieve an important agency mission or performance goal. The employee may receive this credit only upon his or her first appointment as a civilian employee or after reappointment following a 90-day break in service, and if the determination to provide the service credit was made before the employee enters on duty. (5 U.S.C. chapter 6303(e), 5 CFR 630.205)

- Court leave - An employee is entitled to paid time off without charge to leave for service as a juror, and in limited cases, as a witness. An employee is responsible for informing his or her supervisor if he or she is excused from jury or witness service for 1 day or more or for a substantial part of a day. To avoid undue hardship, an agency may adjust the schedule of an employee who works nights or weekends and is called to jury duty. (5 U.S.C. 6322)

- Military leave – There are several different types of military leave entitlements. Under 5 U.S.C. 6323(a) employees performing active duty, active duty training, and inactive duty training are entitled to 15 days of military leave per fiscal year. An employee can carry over a maximum of 15 days into the next fiscal year. Under 5 U.S.C. 6323(b) employees performing emergency duty as ordered by the President, the Secretary of Defense, or a State Governor are entitled to 22 workdays of military leave per calendar year. This leave is provided for employees who perform military duties in support of civil authorities in the protection of life and property or perform full-time military service as a result of a call or order to active duty in support of a contingency operation as defined in section 101(a)(13) of title 10, United States Code. Under 5 U.S.C. 6323(c), employees who are members of the National Guard of the District of Columbia are entitled to unlimited military leave for each day of a parade or encampment ordered or authorized by the commanding general under title 39 of the District of Columbia Code. Under 5 U.S.C. 6323(d), employees who are Reserve and National Guard Technicians (now referred to as military technicians (dual status) are entitled to 44 workdays of military leave in a calendar year when they are on active duty without pay, as authorized pursuant to section 12315 of title 10, under section 12301(b) or 12301(d) of title 10 for participation in operations outside the United States, its territories and possessions. (5 U.S.C. 6323)

- To support Federal employees called to active duty in an Overseas Contingency Operation (formerly the Global War on Terrorism (GWOT)), agencies should grant an employee returning from such active duty 5 work days of excused absence, without charge to leave, immediately upon the employee's return from active duty and prior to his or resumption of work for the agency. In order to receive 5 days of excused absence, an employee must spend at least 42 consecutive days on active duty in support of the Overseas Contingency Operation. Employees are entitled to 5 days of excused absence only once in a 12-month period. A new 12-month period begins after the first use of excused absence. (CPM 2008-21, Minimum Service Requirement to Receive 5 Days of Excused Absence for Employees Returning from Active Military Duty)

4. Job Sharing

Job sharing is an option that may help balance some employees' work and family responsibilities. Under such an arrangement, two employees each work less than full-time, but coordinate their schedules and assignments so together they "share" a work role and ensure the duties and responsibilities of what would otherwise be one full-time position are properly carried out.

5. Employee Assistance Program (EAP)

Contact: Work/Life and Performance Culture at worklife@opm.gov

Although agencies are required by law only to establish and administer employee counseling programs that deal specifically with alcohol and drug abuse, most agencies provide broader services that offer help for a variety of other situations (e.g., work and family pressures, substance abuse or financial difficulties) that can adversely affect work performance and reliability, as well as personal health and well-being.

Generally available to all Federal employees and at no cost to the individual, agency EAPs provide professional and confidential short-term counseling, information, support groups, management consultations, and referrals to extended professional services.

The agency EAPs also play a key role in educating employees on a variety of topics such as money management, parenting, caring for aging parents, stress management, and selecting quality child care.

The basic services provided through the EAP include:

- Confidential, free, short-term counseling to identify and assess the problem(s) and to assist employees in problem solving.

- Referral, where appropriate, to a community service or professional resource that provides treatment and/or rehabilitation. With the exception of illness or injury directly resulting from employment, medical care and treatment are personal to the employee and, therefore, payment may not be made from appropriated funds unless provided for in a contract of employment or by statute or regulation.

- Follow-up services to assist an employee in achieving an effective readjustment to his or her job during and after treatment, e.g., back-to-work conferences.

- Training sessions for managers and supervisors on handling work-related problems that may be related to substance abuse or other personal or health-related problems.

- Orientation and educational programs to familiarize all employees with EAP services and how to access them.

- Briefings to educate management and union officials on the role of the EAP and general consultation on an organizational level, as needed, as in the case of disaster or trauma.

In addition, some agencies have found the EAP to be important in the prevention of, and intervention in, workplace violence incidents, as well as in the delivery of critical-incident stress debriefings and assistance to employees during agency restructuring. For more information go to http://www.opm.gov/policy-data-oversight/worklife/employee-assistance-programs/.

6.   Child and Elder Care Assistance

Contact: Work/Life and Performance Culture at worklife@opm.gov

On-site/Near-site Child Development Centers

Many Federal agencies provide on-site child development centers. There are approximately 1,000 worksite childcare centers sponsored by civilian and military agencies. Valuable resources for assistance include the OPM publication, "Child Care Resources Handbook", www.gsa.gov (search child care) and www.childcare.gov.

Child Care Subsidy

Section 590(g) of title 40, United States Code permits agencies to use appropriated funds to assist their lower-income employees with child care costs. The Federal Child Care Subsidy Program applies to employees whose children (or whose partners' children) are under age 13 (or disabled and under age 18) and are enrolled, or will be enrolled, in family child care homes or center-based child care. The child care provider must be licensed and/or regulated by state and/or local authorities. For more information about this authority, contact Work/Life and Performance Culture or visit http://www.opm.gov/policy-data-oversight/worklife/family-resources/#url=Child-Care-Subsidy. (5 CFR part 792, subpart B)

Dependent Care Flexible Spending Accounts (DCFSA)

A Dependent Care Flexible Spending Account allows an enrollee to use pre-tax wages to pay for eligible dependent care expenses. Eligible expenses are childcare for children under age 13, or day care for anyone who an enrollee can claim as a dependent on a Federal tax return who is physically or mentally incapable of self-care so that the enrollee (and spouse, if married) can work, look for work, or attend school full-time. For more information, see information about Flexible Spending Accounts at http://www.opm.gov/healthcare-insurance/flexible-spending-accounts/ or Family Resources at http://www.opm.gov/policy-data-oversight/worklife/family-resources/#url=Dependent-Care.

Other Child and Elder Care Services

Many agencies offer referral assistance to community resources, provide lunch and learn seminars, and/or sponsor caregiver fairs. The OPM Handbooks for Child and Elder Care Resources, available on the OPM website at http://www.opm.gov/policy-data-oversight/worklife/ in the section "Family Resources", provide employees, managers, and employee assistance counselors with information about organizations and agencies across the country and can help employees locate quality child and elder care services. In addition to any services that agencies may offer, free nationwide resource and referral services can direct callers to local services providers and community resources: (1) Child Care Aware on 1-800-424-2246, and (2) the Elder Care Locator on 1-800-677-1116.

7.   Worksite Health Promotion Programs

 Contact: Work/Life and Performance Culture at worklife@opm.gov

5 U.S.C. 7901 authorizes health services for Federal employees. Federal agencies may establish, within the limits of appropriations available, a health service program to promote and maintain the physical and mental fitness of their Federal employees.Federal agencies currently offer a wide range of preventive health services and programs. Worksite health promotion programs can encourage healthy lifestyle behaviors and complement employee health benefits. Examples of preventive health services and programs include:

• Exercise and physical activity opportunities;
• Diet, nutrition, and eating well;
• Healthy lifestyle education and support;
• Vaccination/immunization; and
• Health screenings.

The OPM website, http://www.opm.gov/policy-data-oversight/worklife/health-wellness/, features guidance for agency program planners as well as an abundance of information designed to enhance the health of Federal employees.

8.   Subsidized Transportation

Federal agencies offer qualified employees a benefit to help defer commuting costs. The benefit applies to all Federal employees who commute to and from work using public transportation and qualified van pools. The program's objectives include improving air quality, reducing traffic congestion, and conserving energy by encouraging employees to commute by means other than single-occupancy vehicles. Employees receive a benefit equal to their actual costs not to exceed an established government-wide limit. The benefit received is not treated as wages for purposes of Federal taxation or withholding and does not have to be reported on a recipient's tax return.

Bicycle Commuter Transportation Subsidies: The Energy Improvement and Extension Act of 2008, in section 211, allows for pre-tax transportation subsidies to cover the cost of reasonable expenses incurred during the calendar year for bicycle commuters. These covered expenses include the purchase of a bicycle and accessories, and for repair and storage of a bicycle that is used regularly for a substantial portion of an employee's commute to and from the workplace.

D.   BENEFITS

1.   Holidays

Additional information on holidays is available at http://www.opm.gov/policy-data-oversight/pay-leave/work-schedules/.

Full-time Federal employees are entitled to ten paid holidays each year. These holidays are specified in 5 U.S.C. 6103 and are listed by year on OPM's website at: http://www.opm.gov/policy-data-oversight/snow-dismissal-procedures/federal-holidays/#url=Overview.
(5 U.S.C. 6103; Executive Order 11582; 5 CFR 610.201 and 610.202)

2.   Life Insurance

Contact: fegli@opm.gov

Eligible full-time and part-time employees are automatically enrolled in the Federal Employees' Group Life Insurance (FEGLI) Program for Basic insurance unless the employee waives it. An employee's Basic Insurance Amount is equal to their salary, rounded to the next even $1,000 plus $2,000, or equal to $10,000, whichever is higher. The cost of FEGLI Basic insurance is shared between the insured individual and the Government. The employee pays two-thirds of the cost and the Government pays one-third of the cost of this group term insurance. New employees do not have to prove insurability, and no physical examination is required. For enrolled employees, accidental death and dismemberment coverage is an automatic part of Basic insurance and Option A (if covered). Employees also can purchase Optional Insurance at their own expense. Optional coverage includes additional insurance on the employee's life, as well as coverage for the employee's spouse and eligible children, if any. Accelerated death benefits (called "Living Benefits") are available to terminally ill enrollees so they can receive their Basic life insurance proceeds while they are living.

Federal Government employees may continue life insurance coverage into retirement if certain requirements are met. It can also be converted to private coverage upon termination without proof of insurability. (5 CFR part 870) See also http://www.opm.gov/healthcare-insurance/life-insurance/.

3.   Health Insurance

Contact: fehb@opm.gov

Unless their position is excluded by law or regulation, Federal employees, including certain temporary employees such as wild-land firefighters can enroll in the Federal Employees Health Benefits (FEHB) Program for themselves and their families at reasonable rates. They enjoy one of the widest plan selections in the country, as there are over 200 health plan choices in the FEHB Program. Employees can choose among fee-for-service plans, health maintenance organizations, and consumer-directed options, including High Deductible Health Plans and Consumer Driven Health Plans. Employees can enroll in the FEHB Program or change their enrollment during the annual open season or upon experiencing a qualifying life event. Federal employees can continue their FEHB coverage into retirement if they retire on an immediate annuity, and were covered for the 5 years of service immediately before retirement or, if less than 5 years, for all years of service in which they were eligible to be enrolled. For annuitants and non-Postal employees, the Government share of the average overall cost of health benefits premiums is about 72 percent. (5 U.S.C. chapter 89) (5 CFR Part 890). See also http://www.opm.gov/healthcare-insurance/healthcare/.

4.   The Federal Employees Dental and Vision Insurance Program

Contact: 1-877-888-FEDS

The Federal Employees Dental and Vision Insurance Program (FEDVIP) offers comprehensive dental and vision insurance to eligible Federal and Postal Service employees, retirees, and their eligible family members on an enrollee-pay-all basis. FEDVIP allows dental and vision insurance to be purchased on a group basis which means competitive premiums and no pre-existing condition limitations. Premiums for enrolled Federal and Postal employees are withheld from the employee's salary on a pre-tax basis. For additional information please visit http://www.opm.gov/healthcare-insurance/dental-vision/.

5.   Pensions

Contact: retire@opm.gov

The Federal Employees Retirement System (FERS) is an outstanding three-tiered plan to provide secure retirement, as well as disability and survivor benefits, for employees appointed to more than one year of service and for their dependents. In addition to Social Security benefits as a base, FERS offers both an annuity that grows with length of service and a tax-deferred savings plan called the Thrift Savings Plan. Employees pay less than one percent of salary to qualify for the annuity and are fully vested after 5 years of service and, for disability benefits, after just 18 months. Employees are eligible to retire at age 62 with 5 or more years of service. After 10 years of service, employees may retire with a reduced annuity at a minimum retirement age that varies according to year of birth (age 57 for those born after 1970), or they may wait until age 62 for full benefits. Employees may retire at age 60 with 20 years service and at the minimum retirement age with 30 years of service. For most retirees, an annuity is calculated at one percent of the high-3 average pay for every year of service. There are enhanced benefits for those who have at least 20 years of service and retire at or after age 62 or for certain positions (for instance, law enforcement officers). (5 CFR part 843) See also http://www.opm.gov/retirement-services/benefits-officers-center/ and http://www.opm.gov/retirement-services/.

There is also a FERS annuity supplement (a special retirement supplement provided to some FERS employees who retire before age 62, because Social Security benefits cannot start before then). The supplement approximates the portion of a full-career Social Security benefit earned while under FERS, and ends at age 62 when Social Security benefits first become available. The supplement is subject to an earnings test.

6.   Thrift Savings Plan

The Thrift Savings Plan (TSP) allows employees to save on a tax-deferred basis for retirement. The TSP permits employees covered by the Federal Employees' Retirement System (FERS) and the Civil Service Retirement System (CSRS) (along with members of the uniformed services) to contribute to the TSP. For FERS employees, the TSP is an integral part of their retirement package, along with FERS Basic Annuity and Social Security. For CSRS employees, the TSP is a supplement to the CSRS annuity. TSP participants can contribute any dollar amount or percentage (1 to 100) of basic pay, however employees hired or rehired after August 2010, are automatically enrolled in the TSP with 3 percent of their pay deducted to contribute to the TSP. The annual maximum contribution to the TSP from pay cannot exceed the Internal Revenue Code (IRC) elective deferral limit, which is $17,000 for 2012. Participants who are age 50 or older may elect an additional deferral to the TSP; catch-up contributions, which cannot exceed IRC limit of $5,500 for 2011. FERS participants are immediately eligible to receive: 1) Agency Automatic (1 percent) Contributions; 2) Agency Matching Contributions of up to 4 percent of basic pay if contributing at least 5 percent of basic pay each pay date. Upon separation from Federal service, FERS employees are immediately vested in Agency Matching Contributions (along with associated earnings) and vested — generally with 3 years of civilian service — in the Agency Automatic (1 percent) Contributions (CSRS participants do not receive any agency contributions).

The TSP is a defined contribution plan. The retirement income from a TSP account will depend on how much the employee (and, if a FERS employee, the agency) have contributed to the employee's account during his or her working years and the earnings on those contributions. Employees can choose to invest in any of ten funds, which include: a Government Securities Investment G Fund, a Fixed Income Index Investment F Fund, a Common Stock Index Investment C Fund, a Small Capitalization Stock Index Investment S Fund, and an International Stock Index Investment I Fund. The TSP also offers five professionally managed Lifecycle (L) Funds which invest in the existing five TSP funds with a portfolio mix designed to invest and shift exposure to risk based on the number of years remaining to invest before using the TSP in a participant's retirement years. The L Funds are named based on the date when the participant would need to begin using their TSP account; L Income (now), L 2020, L 2030, L 2040, L 2050. Also, the new TSP Roth feature gives participants flexibility in the tax treatment of their contributions now and in the future. The Federal Retirement Thrift Investment Board, an independent Federal agency, administers the TSP solely in the interests of the approximately 4.37 million participants and their beneficiaries (5 U.S.C. 8432). See also http://www.tsp.gov.

7.   Long-Term Care Insurance

Contact: LTC@opm.gov

The Long-Term Care Security Act (Public Law 106-265) established the Federal Long Term Care Insurance Program (FLTCIP) in 2000. With passage of the Long-Term Care Security Act, (FLTCIP became the first new benefit offered to Federal employees since the inception of the Federal Employees Retirement System, with its Thrift Savings Plan component, in June 1986. FLTCIP is an important addition to the package of benefits available to the Federal family. Those eligible include Federal and U.S.P.S. employees, annuitants, active and retired members of the military, their spouses and other qualified relatives, including adult children of employees and annuitants, parents and parents-in-law, step parents, and, beginning in 2010, same-sex domestic partners of Federal employees and annuitants. This insurance provides coverage for long-term care services with a focus on helping people continue to live at home. The focus is on helping enrollees with activities of daily living, including dressing, bathing, preparing meals, etc. These services can be provided in a variety of settings including home care, adult day care, assisted living facilities and nursing home care. See also http://www.opm.gov/healthcare-insurance/long-term-care/.

8.   Flexible Spending Accounts

Contact: FSA@opm.gov

There are three types of Flexible Spending Accounts (FSAs). A Health Care FSA (HCFSA) reimburses eligible health care expenses such as co-payments, deductibles, vision and dental expenses and much more. A Limited Expense Health Care FSA (LEX HCFSA) is designed for employees enrolled in or covered by a High Deductible Health Plan with a Health Savings Account. Eligible expenses are limited to dental and vision care expenses which are not covered or reimbursed by FEHBP or FEDVIP coverage or any other insurance. A Dependent Care FSA (DCFSA) will reimburse eligible non-medical day care expenses for the employee's children under age 13 and/or for any person that the employee claims as a dependent on their Federal Income Tax return who is mentally or physically incapable of self-care. All employee contributions to FSAs are made from pre-tax earnings, thereby increasing disposable income. There are no Government contributions to the FSAFEDS program and the employee must enroll anew each open season. The FSAFEDS Open Season is held each fall in conjunction with the FEHB Open Season from mid-November to mid-December. Eligible employees may elect up to $5,000 for a DCFSA and $2,500 for a HCFSA. More information can be found at http://www.opm.gov/healthcare-insurance/flexible-spending-accounts/.

9.   Liability Insurance

Section 642 of Public Law 106-58 requires Federal agencies to reimburse law enforcement officers, supervisors and managers for up to one-half of the cost of professional liability insurance, protecting them from potential liability and attorney's fees for actions arising out of the conduct of official duties.

10.   Severance Pay

Employees may be eligible for severance pay if they serve under a qualifying appointment, have a regularly scheduled tour of duty, have completed at least 12 months of continuous service, and are removed from Federal service by involuntary separation for reasons other than inefficiency (i.e., unacceptable performance or conduct). Additional information on severance pay is available at http://www.opm.gov/policy-data-oversight/pay-leave/pay-administration/fact-sheets/severance-pay/. (5 U.S.C. 5595; 5 CFR part 550, subpart G)

11.   Lump-Sum Annual Leave Payments

An employee will receive a lump-sum payment for any unused annual leave when he or she separates from Federal service or enters active duty in the armed forces and elects to receive a lump-sum payment. Generally, a lump-sum payment will equal the pay the employee would have received had he or she remained employed until expiration of the period covered by the annual leave. Additional information on lump-sum annual leave payments is found at http://www.opm.gov/policy-data-oversight/pay-leave/leave-administration/fact-sheets/lump-sum-payments-for-annual-leave/. (5 U.S.C. 5551; 5 CFR part 550, subpart L)

E.   AGENCY-BASED COMPENSATION FLEXIBILITIES

Agencies have discretionary authority to provide additional direct compensation in certain circumstances to support their recruitment, relocation, and retention efforts. The following summarizes some of these compensation flexibilities. Agencies should ensure that any compensation flexibilities are used judiciously and in accordance with applicable law, regulations, agency policy, and budgetary limitations. Authorities that apply only to the Federal Wage System are grouped together.

Additional information on recruitment, relocation, and retention incentives is available at http://www.opm.gov/policy-data-oversight/pay-leave/recruitment-relocation-retention-incentives/.

1.   Recruitment Incentives

An agency may pay a recruitment incentive to a newly-appointed employee if the agency has determined the position is likely to be difficult to fill in the absence of an incentive. The employee must sign an agreement to complete a specified period of service with the agency (not to exceed 4 years). Total recruitment incentive payments may not exceed 25 percent of the employee's annual rate of basic pay in effect at the beginning of the service period multiplied by the number of years in the service period. (This cap may be increased with OPM approval.) The incentive may be paid as an initial lump-sum payment at the beginning of the service period, in installments throughout the service period, as a final-lump sum payment upon completion of the service period, or in a combination of these payment methods. (5 U.S.C. 5753; 5 CFR part 575, subpart A)

2.   Relocation Incentives

An agency may pay a relocation incentive to a current employee who must relocate to accept a position in a different geographic area if the agency determines the position is likely to be difficult to fill in the absence of an incentive. The employee must sign an agreement to complete a specified period of service with the agency (not to exceed 4 years). Total relocation incentive payments may not exceed 25 percent of the employee's annual rate of basic pay in effect at the beginning of the service period multiplied by the number of years in the service period. (This cap may be increased with OPM approval.) The incentive may be paid as an initial lump-sum payment at the beginning of the service period, in installments throughout the service period, as a final lump-sum payment upon completion of the service period, or in a combination of these payment methods. (5 U.S.C. 5753; 5 CFR part 575, subpart B)

3.   Retention Incentives (likely to leave the Federal service)

An agency may pay a retention incentive to a current employee if the agency determines the unusually high or unique qualifications of the employee or a special need of the agency for the employee's services makes it essential to retain the employee and the employee would be likely to leave the Federal service in the absence of a retention incentive. An agency may also authorize retention incentives for a group or category of employees under these conditions. A retention incentive may not exceed 25 percent of the rate of basic pay for an individual employee or 10 percent for a group or category of employees. (OPM may approve retention incentives in excess of these limits of up to 50 percent of basic pay.) The incentive may be paid in biweekly installments without a service agreement, in other installments after the completion of specified periods of service within the full period of service required by a service agreement, or in a single lump sum after completion of the full period of service required by a service agreement. (5 U.S.C. 5754; 5 CFR part 575, subpart C)

4.   Retention Incentives (likely to leave for a different Federal position)

An agency may pay a retention incentive to a current employee if the agency determines—

- Given the agency's mission requirements and the employee's competencies, the agency has a special need for the employee's services that makes it essential to retain the employee in his or her current position during a period of time before the closure or relocation of the employee's office, facility, activity, or organization; and
- The employee would be likely to leave for a different position in the Federal service in the absence of a retention incentive.

Agencies also may approve a retention incentive under this circumstance for a group or category of employees. (5 U.S.C. 5754; 5 CFR 575.315)

5.   Superior Qualifications and Special Needs Pay-Setting Authority and Special Qualifications Appointments

Agencies may set the rate of basic pay of a newly-appointed employee at a rate above the minimum rate of the appropriate General Schedule (GS) grade because (1) the candidate has superior qualifications or (2) the agency has a special need for the candidate's services. Agencies may use the superior qualifications and special needs pay-setting authority to set the rate of basic pay for an employee upon (1) first appointment as a civilian employee of the Federal Government or (2) reappointment to a GS position with a 90-day break in service. Additional information is available at http://www.opm.gov/policy-data-oversight/pay-leave/pay-administration/fact-sheets/superior-qualifications-and-special-needs-pay-setting-authority/. Under the Federal Wage System, special qualification appointments allow an employing agency to set pay at a rate above step 1 of the appropriate grade level for candidates with highly specialized skills in an occupation. (See 5 U.S.C. 5333 and 5 CFR 531.212 for General Schedule employees. See 5 U.S.C. 5341 and 5 CFR 532.403 for the Federal Wage System.)

6.   Maximum Payable Rate Rule (Highest Previous Rate)

Upon reemployment, transfer, reassignment, promotion, demotion, change in type of appointment, termination of a critical position pay authority under 5 CFR part 535, movement from a non-GS pay system, or termination of grade or pay retention under 5 CFR part 536, an agency may set the rate of basic pay of an employee by taking into account a rate of basic pay previously received by the individual while employed in another civilian Federal position (with certain exceptions). This rate may not exceed the maximum rate of the employee's grade. (See 5 U.S.C. 5334(a), 5 CFR 531.221, and http://www.opm.gov/policy-data-oversight/pay-leave/pay-administration/fact-sheets/maximum-payable-rate-rule/ for General Schedule employees. See 5 U.S.C. 5343 and 5 CFR 532.405 for the Federal Wage System.)

7.   Waiver of Dual Pay Limitation

Contact: Employment Information Office at 202-606-2525

Agencies have authority to waive the limitation (40 hours per week) on aggregate basic pay, when "required services cannot be readily obtained otherwise" and "under emergency conditions relating to health, safety, protection of life or property, or national emergency." This authority enables an agency to employ a full-time Federal employee in a second job or to schedule a part-time agency employee with multiple part-time appointments to work more than an aggregate of 40 hours during a week. The agency pays overtime ONLY when an individual works more than 8 hours per day or 40 hours per week for the SAME agency. (5 U.S.C. 5533; 5 CFR part 550, subpart E)

8.   Travel and Transportation Expenses for Interviews and/or New Appointments

Contact: Employment Information Office at 202-606-2525

An agency, at its discretion, may pay the travel or transportation expenses of any individual candidate for a pre-employment interview or pay travel and transportation expenses for a new appointee to the first post of duty. For either payment, a decision made for one vacancy does not require a like decision for any similar future vacancies. The agency must consider factors such as availability of funds, desirability of conducting interviews, and the feasibility of offering a recruitment incentive before authorizing any payments. (5 U.S.C. 5706b; 5 U.S.C. 5725: 5 CFR part 572)

9. Advances in Pay for New Appointees

Agencies may advance a new hire up to two paychecks so a new employee can pay immediate expenses that are normally incurred as a result of starting a new job and/or relocating to a new geographic area. (5 U.S.C. 5524a; 5 CFR part 550, subpart B)

10. Premium Pay, Exceptions to the Biweekly Limitation

Additional information is available at http://www.opm.gov/policy-data-oversight/pay-leave/pay-administration/#url=Biweekly-Pay-Caps.

The head of an agency (or designee) may make an exception to the biweekly limitation on premium pay during emergencies involving a direct threat to life or property or in mission-critical situations. If the head of an agency determines such an emergency exists or an employee is needed to perform mission-critical work, the premium pay paid to an employee performing work in connection with that emergency or mission-critical situation, when added to the employee's basic pay (including any locality payment or special rate supplement) for the calendar year, must not cause his or her total pay to exceed the **greater** of the annual rate payable for (1) GS-15, step 10 (including any locality payment or special rate supplement) in effect on the last day of the calendar year, or (2) the annual rate payable for level V of the Executive Schedule in effect on the last day of the calendar year. Certain types of premium pay remain subject to a biweekly limitation when other premium payments are subject to an annual limitation. (Note: This limitation does not apply to overtime pay earned under the Fair Labor Standards Act. This limitation does not apply to the Federal Wage System.) (5 U.S.C. 5547(b); 5 CFR 550.106-107)

11. Supervisory Differential

The head of an agency may pay a supervisory differential to a General Schedule employee who has supervisory responsibility for one or more civilian employees not covered by the General Schedule if one or more of the subordinate civilian employees, in the absence of such a differential, would be paid more than the supervisory employee. (5 U.S.C. 5755; 5 CFR part 575, subpart D)

12. Student Loan Repayment Program

Using this authority, agencies may repay certain types of Federally made, insured, or guaranteed student loans to attract job candidates or retain current employees. The program implements 5 U.S.C. 5379, which authorizes agencies to set up their own loan repayment programs to attract or retain highly qualified employees. Individuals interested in student loan repayment opportunities must contact agencies directly. Agencies may make payments to the loan holder of up to a maximum of $10,000 for an employee in a calendar year and a total of not more than $60,000 for any one employee. In return, employees must sign a service agreement to remain in the service of the paying agency for a period of at least 3 years. Please see http://www.opm.gov/policy-data-oversight/pay-leave/student-loan-repayment/ for more information. (5 U.S.C. 5379; 5 CFR part 537)

13.   Combat Zone

Special pay and benefits apply to eligible civilian Federal employees assigned to duty in certain combat zones such as Iraq and Afghanistan. The Department of Defense, the Department of State, and the Department of Labor administer many of the pay and benefits programs provided to Federal civilian employees working in overseas locations, including combat zones. Pay and benefits may vary depending on the employee's pay system, assignment location, scope and nature of duties, and nature of assignment. Please see http://www.opm.gov/combatzones for more information.

F.   *COMPENSATION FLEXIBILITIES AVAILABLE WITH OPM AND/OR OMB APPROVAL*

1.   Special Rates

Additional information on special rates is available at http://apps.opm.gov/SpecialRates/index.asp

OPM may establish higher rates of pay for an occupation or group of occupations nationwide, worldwide, or in a local area when it finds that the Government's recruitment or retention efforts are, or would likely become, significantly handicapped without those higher rates. The minimum rate of a special rate range may exceed the maximum rate of the corresponding grade by as much as 30 percent. However, no special rate may exceed the rate for Executive Level IV. A special rate request must be submitted to OPM by an agency's headquarters and must be coordinated with other Federal agencies with employees in the same occupational group and geographic area. (5 U.S.C. 5305; 5 CFR part 530, subpart C)

2.   Recruitment and Relocation Incentives in Excess of 25 Percent

Upon the request of the head of an agency, OPM may waive the recruitment or relocation incentive 25 percent limitation based on a critical agency need. Under such an approval, the total amount of recruitment or relocation incentive payments may not exceed 50 percent of an employee's annual rate of basic pay at the beginning of the service period multiplied by the number of years in the service period. In no event may a waiver provide total recruitment or relocation incentive payments exceeding 100 percent of an employee's annual rate of basic pay at the beginning of the service period. The agency must determine that the competencies required for the position are critical to the successful accomplishment of an important agency mission, project or initiative (e.g., programs or projects related to a national emergency or implementing a new law or critical management initiative). (5 U.S.C. 5753; 5 CFR part 575, subparts A and B)

3.   Retention Incentives in Excess of 25 Percent for Individual Employees and 10 Percent for Groups of Employees

At the request of an agency head, OPM may waive the retention incentive limitation of 25 percent of basic pay for individual employees or 10 percent for a group or category of employees (but not to exceed 50 percent of basic pay) based on a critical agency need.   The agency must determine the unusually high or unique qualifications of the employee(s) are critical to the successful accomplishment of an important agency mission, project or initiative (e.g., programs or projects related to a national emergency or implementing a new law or critical management initiative). (5 U.S.C. 5754; 5 CFR part 575, subpart C)

4.   Critical Position Pay Authority

OPM may, upon the request of an agency head, and after consultation with the Office of Management and Budget (OMB), grant authority to fix the rate of basic pay for one or more critical positions in an agency at not less than the rate that would otherwise be payable for that position, up to the rate for level I of the Executive Schedule under the critical pay authority. Under this same provision of law, a higher rate of pay may be established upon the President's written approval. To apply the critical pay authority, the position must require a very high level of expertise in a scientific, technical, professional, or administrative field and be crucial to the accomplishment of an agency's mission. (5 U.S.C. 5377; OMB Bulletin No. 91-09)

5.   Physicians Comparability Allowance

Physicians comparability allowances (PCAs) may be paid to certain eligible Federal physicians who enter into service agreements with their agencies. These allowances are paid only to categories of physicians for which the agency is experiencing recruitment and retention problems and are fixed at the minimum amounts necessary to deal with such problems. Agencies may pay a physicians comparability allowance of up to $14,000 annually to a physician with 24 months or less of service as a Government physician. Agencies may pay a physicians comparability allowance of up to $30,000 annually to a physician with more than 24 months of service as a Government physician. An agency plan for implementing the PCA program must be approved by the Office of Management and Budget before an agency may pay a PCA to a physician. (5 U.S.C. 5948; 5 CFR part 595)

6.   Title 38 Flexibilities for Health Care Employees

At the request of an agency head, OPM may delegate the discretionary use of certain Department of Veterans Affairs personnel authorities under 38 U.S.C. chapter 74 to help recruit and retain employees in health care occupations. OPM has entered into title 38 delegation agreements with the Departments of Defense, Health and Human Services, Justice, Homeland Security, and Veterans Affairs and the Armed Forces Retirement Home for employees covered under 5 U.S.C. chapter 51 (excluding members of the Senior Executive Service) performing direct patient-care services or services incident to direct patient care. Under these delegation agreements, agencies may establish and use certain title 38 authorities such as the special rates, premium pay, qualifications-based grading system, and physician and dentist pay authorities. (5 U.S.C. 5371)

7.   Federal Wage System Authorities

Additional information on the Federal Wage System is available at http://www.opm.gov/policy-data-oversight/pay-leave/pay-systems/federal-wage-system/.

- Special Rates - The special rate authority allows a lead agency, with the approval of OPM, to establish rates above the regular Federal Wage System wage schedule rates for an occupation or group of occupations experiencing or potentially experiencing recruitment or retention difficulties. Special rates are established by occupation, grade, agency, and/or geographic location. These rates will be paid by all agencies having positions for which the rates are authorized. The special rate payable may not, at any time, be less than the unrestricted rate otherwise payable for such positions under the applicable regular wage schedule. (5 U.S.C. 5341; 5 CFR 532.251)

- Increased Minimum Hiring Rate - The increased minimum hiring rate authority allows a lead agency to establish any Federal Wage System scheduled rate above step 1 as the minimum rate at which a new employee can be hired. When there is an increased minimum rate authorization for an occupation and grade at a particular location, all appointments must be made at the authorized increased minimum rate. (5 U.S.C. 5341; 5 CFR 532.249)

- Special Schedules - The special schedule authority allows a lead agency, with the approval of OPM, to establish a Federal Wage System schedule of rates broader in scope than would normally be authorized under the special rates program. Special schedules are established to ensure the recruitment or retention of qualified employees or to address unique agency missions or other unusual circumstances. Special schedules are established for specific occupations within a geographic area. (5 U.S.C. 5341; 5 CFR 532.254)

- Unrestricted Rate Authority - OPM may approve exceptions to a statutory limitation on Federal Wage System pay adjustments for an occupation or group of occupations in a wage area or part of a wage area upon the request of an agency if such exceptions are necessary to ensure the recruitment or retention of qualified employees. The lead agency for the wage area must coordinate with other agencies, as necessary, an employing agency's request for this exception and submit a consolidated request to OPM. The consolidated request must include any available supporting wage survey data and a formal recommendation by the lead agency to approve or disapprove the request. (Requires specific authority in annual pay limitation legislation, as applicable; see 5 CFR 532.801.)

G.   *PREMIUM PAY AND ALLOWANCES*

Additional information on premium pay is available at http://www.opm.gov/policy-data-oversight/pay-leave/pay-administration/#url=Fact-Sheets.

1.   Overtime Pay or Compensatory Time Off

Overtime pay or compensatory time off is generally earned for hours of work officially ordered or approved in excess of 8 hours in a day or 40 hours in an administrative workweek. For employees on compressed work schedules overtime pay is for hours of work in excess of the compressed work schedule. For employees on flexible work schedules, overtime hours are generally for work officially ordered in advance beyond 80 hours per biweekly pay period (i.e., beyond the 80-hour biweekly basic work requirement). Additional information on overtime pay under title 5, United States Code, for FLSA-exempt employees can be obtained at http://www.opm.gov/policy-data-oversight/pay-leave/pay-administration/fact-sheets/overtime-pay-title-5/. Information on overtime pay under the Fair Labor Standards Act for FLSA-nonexempt employees is in 5 CFR part 551.

Information on compensatory time off can be obtained at   http://www.opm.gov/policy-data-oversight/pay-leave/pay-administration/fact-sheets/compensatory-time-off/ and information on hours of work for travel can be found at http://www.opm.gov/policy-data-oversight/pay-leave/work-schedules/fact-sheets/hours-of-work-for-travel/. (5 U.S.C. 5542 and 5543; 29 U.S.C. 201 et seq; 5 CFR part 550, subpart A, and 5 CFR part 551, subpart E) Further details on overtime pay and compensatory time off for FLSA-exempt and non-exempt employees may also be found at http://www.chcoc.gov/Transmittals/TransmittalDetails.aspx?TransmittalId=2425.

2.   Night Pay

Generally, General Schedule employees regularly scheduled to work between the hours of 6 p.m. and 6 a.m. are entitled to night pay. Employees receive night pay for work performed during these hours (including paid holidays) and for periods of paid leave when the total amount of leave taken is less than 8 hours during the pay period. Premium pay for night work equals 10 percent of the employee's rate of basic pay. Please see http://www.opm.gov/policy-data-oversight/pay-leave/pay-administration/fact-sheets/night-pay-for-general-schedule-employees/ for more information. (5 U.S.C. 5545(a); 5 CFR 550.121-122)

3.   Night Shift Differential

A prevailing rate employee is entitled to pay at his or her scheduled rate plus a differential of 7 ½ percent of the scheduled rate for regularly scheduled non-overtime work when the majority of the employee's work hours occur between 3 p.m. and midnight. Employees are entitled to 10 percent of the employee's scheduled rate for regularly scheduled non-overtime work if the majority of the employee's work hours occur between 11 p.m. and 8 a.m. Night shift differential is paid for the entire shift when the majority of hours fall within the specified periods. Please see http://www.opm.gov/policy-data-oversight/pay-leave/pay-administration/fact-sheets/night-shift-differential-for-federal-wage-system-employees/ for more information. (5 U.S.C. 5343(f); 5 CFR 532.505)

4.   Sunday Premium Pay

An employee who performs up to 8 hours of regularly scheduled non-overtime work during a tour of duty, any part of which occurs on Sunday, is entitled to premium pay for the entire tour of duty equal to 25 percent of the employee's rate of basic pay. Sunday premium pay is not paid when Sunday work is not actually performed, including during leave hours. Employees on compressed work schedules are paid for the number of regularly scheduled non-overtime hours worked in a tour of duty that begins or ends on a Sunday. Please see http://www.opm.gov/policy-data-oversight/pay-leave/pay-administration/fact-sheets/sunday-premium-pay/ for more information. (5 U.S.C. 5546(a) and 6128(c); 5 CFR 550.171-172)

5.   Holiday Premium Pay

Most Federal employees who perform non-overtime work on a holiday are entitled to pay at their rate of basic pay plus premium pay at a rate equal to their rate of basic pay for holiday work not in excess of 8 hours (or the number of non-overtime hours under a compressed work schedule on the holiday). Employees assigned to duty on a holiday are entitled to pay for at least 2 hours of holiday work. Additional information on holidays can be found at http://www.opm.gov/policy-data-oversight/pay-leave/pay-administration/fact-sheets/holidays-work-schedules-and-pay. (5 U.S.C. 5546(b), 6103, 6104, 6124 and 6128(d); 5 CFR 550.103, 550.131 and 550.132, 610.201, 610.202, and 610.405-407)

6.   Types of Annual Premium Pay

An agency may pay premium pay on an annual basis to employees in positions that involve substantial amounts of overtime work. Annual premium pay cannot exceed 25 percent of basic pay.

- Standby Duty Pay - May be paid to an employee in a position requiring him or her to regularly remain at, or within the confines of, his or her duty station for more than 40 hours per week, a substantial part of which consists of remaining in a standby status rather than performing work. (5 U.S.C. 5545(c)(1); 5 CFR 550.141-144, 550.161-164)

- Administratively Uncontrollable Overtime Pay - May be paid to an employee in a position in which the hours of duty cannot be controlled administratively and which requires substantial amounts of irregular or occasional overtime work. (5 U.S.C. 5545(c)(2); 5 CFR 550.151-154, 550.161-164)

- Availability Pay for Law Enforcement Officers - Paid to criminal investigators required to work, or be available to work, substantial amounts of "unscheduled duty." (5 U.S.C. 5542(d) and 5545a; 5 CFR 550.181-187)

7.   Hazardous Duty Pay

General Schedule employees may receive additional pay for the performance of hazardous duty or duty involving physical hardship. (5 U.S.C. 5545(d); 5 CFR part 550, subpart I)

8.   Environmental Differential Pay

Prevailing rate (wage) employees may receive an environmental differential when exposed to a working condition, physical hardship, or hazard of an unusually severe nature. (5 U.S.C. 5343(c)(4); 5 CFR 532.511)

9.   Pay for Federal Firefighters

Most Federal firefighters are subject to special pay computation rules that take into account their unusual work schedules. These rules deal with both basic pay and premium pay. (5 U.S.C. 5545b and 5542(f); 5 CFR part 550, subpart M)

10.   Cost-of-living Allowance and/or Post Differential in a Nonforeign Area

Additional information is available at http://www.opm.gov/policy-data-oversight/pay-leave/pay-systems/nonforeign-areas/.

White-collar civilian employees receive a cost-of-living allowance (COLA) when stationed in certain nonforeign areas outside the continental United States (i.e., Alaska, Hawaii, Guam and the Northern Mariana Islands, Puerto Rico, and the U.S. Virgin Islands). COLA payments in the nonforeign areas are based on living costs substantially higher than in the Washington, DC, area. Following passage of the Nonforeign Area Retirement Equity Assurance Act (NAREAA) of 2010, COLA rates were frozen in each nonforeign area, and except for U.S. Postal Service employees, they are being offset and gradually phased-out by General Schedule locality pay to provide pay consistency and retirement equity among Federal employees throughout the United States and the nonforeign areas. COLA will continue to be paid in each nonforeign area until locality pay completely replaces COLA payments.

11.   Post Differential

Some employees in certain nonforeign areas receive a post differential based on environmental conditions that differ substantially from those in the continental United States and which warrant the differential as a recruitment incentive. The post differential is available only to employees recruited from outside the differential area. The maximum amount of the allowance or differential, or their combined total, cannot exceed 25 percent of the hourly rate of basic pay. (5 U.S.C. 5941; 5 CFR part 591, subpart B) Additional information is available at http://www.opm.gov/policy-data-oversight/pay-leave/pay-systems/nonforeign-areas/cola.pdf.

12. Compensatory Time Off for Travel

Additional information is available at http://www.opm.gov/policy-data-oversight/pay-leave/pay-administration/fact-sheets/compensatory-time-off-for-travel/.

Compensatory time off for travel is earned by an employee for time spent in a travel status away from the employee's official duty station when such time is not otherwise compensable. (5 U.S.C. 5550b; 5 CFR part 550, subpart N)

13. Other Payments and Allowances

General Schedule and other specified categories of employees may receive allowances for working in remote worksites or for the expense of a uniform when legal and regulatory requirements are met. In addition, civilian employees may receive advance payments, evacuation payments, and special allowances, in the event of an order to evacuate due to natural disasters or other reasons that create imminent danger to the lives of the employees or their family members. (5 U.S.C. 5942, 5 CFR part 591, subpart C (Remote Worksite Allowance); 5 U.S.C. 5901-5903, 5 CFR part 591, subpart A (Uniform Allowance); and 5 U.S.C. 5522-5524; 5 CFR part 550, subpart D (Evacuation Payments))

Additional information on payments for employees ordered to evacuate is available at http://www.opm.gov/policy-data-oversight/pay-leave/pay-administration/fact-sheets/evacuation-payments/.

H. WORK DESIGN & CLASSIFICATION

Agency managers are responsible and accountable for organizing work in an efficient, effective manner, and for optimizing resources to carry out the missions of their organizations. Under Title 5, managers have broad authority to organize and assign work. This is an area of enormous flexibility guided by more general concepts and practices associated with modern organizational and business management.

1. Work Design

Managers cannot afford to design work in a haphazard manner in today's environment of limited resources. Recent trends in work design indicate a growing shift away from multi-layered, steeply hierarchical organizations to more flexible and flatter organizational structures where teams are accountable for accomplishing the work. These concepts of work or organizational design, also known as "position management," are closely related to classification; i.e., they go hand in hand.

Good position management can be defined as a carefully designed position structure which blends the skills and assignments of employees with the goal of successfully carrying out the organization's mission or program. Sound position management reflects a logical balance between employees needed to carry out the major functions of the organization and those needed to provide adequate support; between professional employees and technicians; between fully trained employees and trainees; and between supervisors and subordinates.

2.   Classification

OPM issues classification and job-grading standards that provide occupational information and grading criteria for positions covered under the standard Governmentwide classification systems (i.e., General Schedule and Federal Wage System) after consulting with agencies.   Agencies use these standards to determine the proper pay plan, occupational series, position title, and grade of each position. Classification is closely related to compensation in the Federal Government because, under the General Schedule, including white-collar occupations and the Federal Wage System, which covers trades, crafts, and labor occupations, the determination of a position's correct grade directly translates to a prescribed rate schedule for basic pay.

Positions in some agencies are not covered under these standard Governmentwide classification systems. For these positions, agency guidance provides information on classifying positions covered under alternative legislative authorities.

Agencies may use various administrative flexibilities to increase the classification systems' effectiveness in responding to organizational changes and workload shifts. OPM provides policies, concepts, and related manuals and handbooks to help agencies meet their mission needs, and assist agency managers in effectively designing work and classifying positions.

These materials are available on OPM's web site (http://www.opm.gov/policy-data-oversight/classification-qualifications/). They include:

Guidance for General Schedule Positions:
- Handbook of Occupational Groups and Families (Part I)
- Introduction to the Position Classification Standards
- The Classifier's Handbook
- Position Classification Standards (including Job Family Standards)
- Functional Guides
- Recent Issuances in Federal Classification

Guidance for Federal Wage System Positions:
- Handbook of Occupational Groups and Families (Part II)
- Introduction to the Federal Wage System Job Grading System
- Job Grading Standards
- Functional Standards

Job family standards (JFSs) are broad position classification standards that cover an entire area or family of related work rather than an individual occupational series or specialty. OPM is in the process of replacing numerous occupational standards for General Schedule series with more streamlined job family standards. JFSs acknowledge distinctions among the work within the family, as appropriate. They sometimes consolidate occupational series, if the work changes to that extent, and sometimes describe individual series, depending upon the results of the occupational research. JFSs simplify classification for the user, because the user can refer to a single standard to evaluate related work.

Recently developed classification standards provide agencies with up-to-date occupational information and grading criteria agency managers can use to help organize and design work, establish positions, and facilitate recruitment actions.

Classification standards may authorize parenthetical specialty titles to facilitate targeted recruitment and self-identification, thus leading to more efficient recruiting and selection.

All position classification standards and functional classification guides are available on the Internet. Users may access both current standards and draft standards that are under development at http://www.opm.gov/policy-data-oversight/classification-qualifications/.

On-Line Technical Assistance. Agency managers, employees, and specifically classification staffs, have also found OPM's on-line technical assistance inquiry system to be of tremendous help in getting quick answers to questions, particularly about their specific work design or classification situations. It has proven to be an excellent management tool. Since inception, the new system, "Fedclass", has provided a vast amount of informal advice and technical assistance. Contact the following address for online technical assistance: fedclass@opm.gov

On-Line Classification Community: Managers and classifiers may find this web community a valuable information exchange center.
Visit http://max.omb.gov/community/display/HumanCapital/classification.

3.   Automated Procedures

Use of automated procedures has streamlined the development of position descriptions and the evaluation of positions. Many agencies have purchased commercial automated classification systems. Others are using internally developed systems. Agencies using such systems continue to be responsible for the quality of their position descriptions and classification decisions and for compliance with relevant policy requirements. Automated systems are not substitutes for proper classification; rather they can serve to supplement, facilitate, and enhance not only agency classification efforts, but also staffing, performance management, human resource development, employee relations, and labor relations.

4.   Delayering Support

The General Schedule Supervisory Guide (GSSG) provides guidance for determining a supervisory position, as well as setting supervisory grade levels. The guidance makes clear workload is considered in determining whether a position is supervisory. This reinforces the goal of delayering and avoiding hierarchical fragmentation. The GSSG does not specify number of people supervised as a factor in setting supervisory grade levels. In addition to the GSSG, the General Schedule Leader Grade Evaluation Guide provides guidance for positions that manage clerical or other one-grade interval positions. Both guides provide agencies flexibility in staffing teams to meet agency goals.

- General Schedule Supervisory Guide (http://www.opm.gov/policy-data-oversight/classification-qualifications/classifying-general-schedule-positions/functional-guides/gssg.pdf)

- General Schedule Leader Grade Evaluation Guide (http://www.opm.gov/policy-data-oversight/classification-qualifications/classifying-general-schedule-positions/functional-guides/gslead.pdf)

5.   Job Redesign

Sometimes positions are difficult to fill because the pool of available candidates lacks a particular skill or competency for the job, or conversely, has higher-level skills that pay more in the private sector. Agency managers have the authority and discretion to redesign a position by eliminating or adding higher-level job duties to better match available candidates. Agencies may also redesign jobs to make them more appealing to candidates by adding desirable duties and eliminating undesirable duties. It is important to note that job redesign should be done within the framework of the organization's mission and work functions. Duties should not be applied that are not going to be performed on the job, and should not result in grade levels that exceed what is needed to perform the work of the unit.

6.   Upward Mobility Positions

Upward mobility positions may be increasingly important in an era where competition for talent is keen. Managers can structure new and vacant positions to allow entry at lower levels from the current workforce, thereby encouraging high performance and rewarding excellence with greater opportunity. Structured training and experience features must be developed and carefully monitored to ensure success of employees selected for upward mobility positions.

7.   Work Design Concepts or "Rules of Thumb"

- Assign responsibility to line managers at appropriate levels and accountability in the organization.

- Determine the "right" span of control for supervisors in the organization; i.e., the number and grade levels of employees one supervisor can effectively manage.

- Use team leaders rather than supervisors when practical to facilitate work.

- Plan positions so there are logical entrance levels, and logical career patterns for progression to more skilled and higher-grade positions as employees gain skill and ability to assume greater responsibility.

I.   *PERFORMANCE MANAGEMENT*

The governing statute and OPM performance management regulations establish a broad framework for designing performance appraisal and awards programs. This broad framework allows agencies to develop performance management programs that help them achieve their goals, improve organizational performance, and create a high-performance climate that attracts and retains top performers. A number of agencies have developed successful performance management programs. OPM describes many of those programs in its Performance Management Clearinghouse, an online database that includes descriptions of effective Federal performance management programs, processes, and practices.

"Performance management" in the context of human resources authorities is intended to relate to the management of employee performance (i.e., planning, monitoring, developing, rating, and rewarding employee contributions), rather than performance-oriented approaches to managing, measuring, and accounting for agency program performance. Organizational performance management should link to employee performance management. For example, agencies should ensure they align employee performance plans with the agency strategic and annual performance plans required by the Government Performance and Results Modernization Act of 2010. Although organizational performance should inform employee performance management, the two remain distinct in some respects, particularly regarding establishing individual accountability and dealing with poor performers. (5 CFR part 430, subpart B)

For general questions, visit OPM's Performance Management Technical Assistance Center at http://www.opm.gov/policy-data-oversight/performance-management/.

1.   Performance Planning and Appraisal

Within a broad framework, the governing statute and performance management regulations give agencies the freedom to choose the design of their appraisal systems and programs. Design issues include the following:

- An agency can establish an overarching performance appraisal system that allows its components to design a variety of appraisal programs, or requires one program for all its employees, or is some variation of these options.

- Appraisal programs can use as few as two and as many as five summary rating levels in official ratings of record.

- OPM's regulations require each employee's performance plan include at least one critical element, which, by definition, measures individual performance and establishes individual accountability. However, appraisal programs can also include non-critical and additional performance elements, which can measure individual, group, or organizational performance.

- Agencies can take group and organizational performance into account, as appropriate, when assigning ratings of record above Unacceptable.

2.   Incentive Awards and Recognition

Agencies have authority to design extensive awards programs that include cash awards, honorary awards, informal recognition awards, and time-off awards. Agencies can give these awards to Federal employees to recognize employee and group performance, and can design incentive programs with awards granted because an individual or a group achieved pre-established goals. OPM award regulations allow the following:

- Rating-Based Cash Awards - Agencies have discretionary authority to grant an employee a lump-sum cash award based on a "Fully Successful" or better rating of record. Cash awards do not increase an employee's basic pay. Awards based on the rating of record can be up to 10 percent of salary, or up to 20 percent for exceptional performance. (5 U.S.C. 4302, 4503, 4505a; 5 CFR 451.104)

- Other Cash Awards - Agencies may grant a cash award to an employee, individually or as a member of a group, in recognition of accomplishments that contribute to the efficiency, economy, or other improvement of Government operations. Agencies may grant up to $10,000 without external approval, up to $25,000 with OPM approval, and in excess of $25,000 with Presidential approval. (The Department of Defense and the Internal Revenue Service do not require OPM approval for awards up to $25,000, but the President must approve awards over $25,000 after review and approval by OPM.) Award payments are subject to the aggregate limitation on total pay equal to the rate of pay for Executive Level I. For senior-level and scientific or professional employees (as for members of the Senior Executive Service), this aggregate limitation on total pay is equal to the rate of the Vice President's salary when they are covered by a performance appraisal system that has been certified as making meaningful distinctions based on relative performance. (5 U.S.C. chapter 45; 5 CFR part 451 and 5 U.S.C. 5307(d); 5 CFR part 530, subpart B)

- Referral Bonuses - Federal agencies can use the incentive awards authority under chapter 45, title 5, U.S. Code, to provide incentives or recognition to employees who bring new talent into the agency, usually by establishing a specific award such as a referral bonus. Each agency must determine whether the use of referral bonuses is appropriate and establish criteria for giving them to employees. These incentive programs must not violate legal requirements for broad public awareness of job openings; recruitment from appropriate sources to seek a workforce drawn from all segments of society; and hiring selections based solely on relative ability, knowledge, and skills after a fair and open competition that assures all candidates receive equal opportunity. (5 U.S.C. 2301 (b) (1), (b) (2); 5 CFR 2.1 (a), 4.2, 451.106)

  In addition, consistent with OPM's policy on recruitment incentives under the Federal Workforce Flexibility Act of 2004, referral bonuses should not be paid for interagency recruiting within a geographic area.

- Quality Step Increases - Agencies have discretionary authority to accelerate an employee's advancement through the steps of his or her General Schedule grade by granting a quality step increase. A quality step increase is an additional step increase that agencies may grant to an employee who has received the highest rating of record available under the applicable performance appraisal program, which would be "Outstanding" or Level 5 if such a level is available, and has met the agency-developed additional criteria required for programs that do not use a Level 5 summary. Quality step increases are basic pay increases for all purposes. Agencies can grant no more than one quality step increase to an employee within a 52-week period, and such an increase may not cause the employee's pay to exceed the maximum rate of the grade. There is no authority to grant quality step increases to Federal Wage System employees. (5 U.S.C. 5336; 5 CFR part 531, subpart E)

- Honorary and Informal Recognition Awards - Agencies can develop honorary and informal recognition programs that use recognition items as awards to recognize individual and group performance. Recognition items must meet certain criteria. Honorary awards: a) must be something that the recipient could reasonably be expected to value, but not something that conveys a sense of monetary value; b) must have a lasting trophy value; c) must clearly symbolize the employer-employee relationship in some fashion; and d) must take an appropriate form to be used in the public sector and to be purchased with public funds. (5 U.S.C. 4503; 5 CFR 451.104(a))

  Informal recognition awards: a) must be of nominal value; and b) must take an appropriate form to be used in the public sector and to be purchased with public funds. (5 U.S.C. 4503; 5 CFR 451.104(a))

  For additional information on using "Nonmonetary Items" as Incentive Awards, go to http://www.opm.gov/policy-data-oversight/performance-management/performance-management-cycle/rewarding/using-nonmonetary-items-as-incentive-awards/.

- Time-Off Awards - Agencies may grant time off from duty without charge to leave or loss of pay as an award to individuals or groups of employees. (5 U.S.C. 4502; 5 CFR part 451)

3.   Results-Oriented Performance Culture

As mentioned in Section B, the need for strategic human capital management, with its emphasis on achieving results, is part of a continuing evolution of traditional HRM practices in the Government. Information on building and sustaining a results-oriented performance culture may be found at http://www.opm.gov/policy-data-oversight/human-capital-management/performance-culture/.

The Results-Oriented Performance Culture system is described in the HCAAF Resource Center and has detailed information on critical success factors that work together to create a diverse, results-oriented, high performance workforce. The factors include:

- Communication
- Performance Appraisal
- Awards
- Pay-for-Performance
- Diversity Management
- Labor/Management Relations

4.   Alternative Personnel Systems and Demonstration Projects

The term Alternative Personnel Systems (APS) is applied when agencies choose to look outside of traditional personnel systems (e.g. General Schedule) to address longstanding human resources issues. OPM has worked with agencies for over 30 years to implement APSs. Most of those systems have fallen under OPM's demonstration project oversight authority and have had some element of performance-based pay. Information on existing APSs, including specific demonstration projects can be found at www.opm.gov/aps/.

A demonstration project provides a means for testing and introducing beneficial change in Government-wide human resources management systems. A Federal agency obtains the authority from OPM to waive existing Federal human resources management law and regulations in title 5, United States Code, and title 5, Code of Federal Regulations, to propose, develop, test, and evaluate interventions for its own human resources management system. No waivers of law are permitted in areas of employee leave, employee benefits, equal employment opportunity, political activity, merit system principles, or other prohibited personnel practices. Examples of laws and regulations that may be waived under title 5 include:

- qualification requirements, recruitment, and appointment to positions;
- classification and compensation;
- assignment, reassignment, or promotions;
- disciplinary actions;
- providing incentives;
- establishing hours of work;
- involving employees and labor organizations in personnel decisions; and
- reducing overall agency staff and grade levels.

J.   *TRAINING & DEVELOPMENT*

1.   Establishment of Training Programs

To assist in achieving an agency's mission and performance goals by improving employee and organizational performance, the law prescribes that "the head of each agency, in conformity with this chapter, shall establish, operate, maintain, and evaluate a program or programs, and a plan or plans thereunder, for the training of employees in or under the agency by, in, and through Government facilities and non-Government facilities." (5 U.S.C. 4103(a))

- Tuition Reimbursement Programs - Agencies may offer employees financial assistance to attend academic courses that are job related.

- Targeted Career Training - A centralized effort is used to provide effective and consistent HR training at grades 5-15, which combines formal coursework with rotations, and is based upon defined competencies in an HR Career Program. The program design provides professional, technical and leadership training for all aspects of workforce management recruitment, retention and development.

- Professional Development - Another professional development program for career employees is designed to provide technical and general knowledge and experience. The program includes well-rounded orientation consisting of formal coursework and on-the-job training assignments throughout the agency.

2.   Individual Learning Accounts

Individual Learning Accounts (ILAs) can complement current agency development, recruitment, and retention activities. The objectives of agency ILAs include:

- Improving organizational performance.
- Meeting specific agency performance goals.
- Increasing employee access to and use of emerging learning technology.
- Supporting employee efforts to acquire skills and learning needed to succeed in specific occupations and professions.
- Providing employees with flexible learning opportunities and putting the responsibility for learning in the hands of the learner.

ILAs can improve overall Federal employee performance by increasing productivity and improving customer service skills. They offer Federal employees an additional chance to develop themselves and can enhance agencies' ability to remain competitive in the global job market and to attract the very best candidates for Federal positions.

Detailed information about results of the Federal ILA Pilot and how to implement agency ILAs can be found at http://www.opm.gov/hrd/lead/ILA/ilarpind.htm. More information on ILA's and successful implementation of ILA programs can be found on the ILA page on the OPM Training and Development Wiki.

3.   Training and Education Related to an Employee's Official Duties

- Development Opportunities - Employees may be assigned to state and local governments, colleges and universities, Indian tribal organizations, and other not-for-profit organizations under the Intergovernmental Personnel Act (IPA) Mobility Program. Such assignments should be for the mutual benefit of the Federal Government and the non-Federal entity, and can be used to provide program and developmental experience that will enhance the assignee's performance in his or her permanent Federal job. Assignments are for 2 years; however, they can be extended for an additional 2 years, allowing for a maximum term of 4 consecutive years. Cost-sharing arrangements for mobility assignments are negotiated between the participating organizations. The Federal agency may agree to pay all, some, or none of the costs associated with the assignment. Such costs may include basic pay, supplemental pay, benefits, and travel and relocation expenses. (5 U.S.C. 3371-3375; 5 CFR part 334)

- Paying Costs of Training and Education from Program Funds - Agencies may pay training and education expenses from appropriated funds or other available funds. Program funds may be used to pay for training needed to support program functions. (5 U.S.C. 4112, 5 CFR 410.304)

- Paying Costs of Training and Education In Advance - Agencies may pay a vendor the costs of training or education in advance. They may also advance an employee all or part of the costs of approved training and education. Expenses of training include the cost of tuition; purchase or rental of books, materials and supplies; library and laboratory fees; and travel, per diem, and relocation expenses. (5 U.S.C 4109(a)(2))

- Reimbursing Employees for Training and Education Costs - An agency may reimburse employees for all or part of the costs of training or education. Expenses of training include the cost of tuition; purchase or rental of books, materials, and supplies; library and laboratory fees; and travel, per diem, and relocation expenses. (5 U.S.C. 4109(a)(2))

- Sharing the Costs of Training and Education with Employees - Agencies may share training and education costs with employees. This authority allows agencies to support training and education that benefits both the agency and the employee. (5 U.S.C. 4109(a)(2))

The following table illustrates the variety of arrangements that agencies and employees may use to share training costs and accommodate schedules as well as the organization's and the employee's needs.

Paying Training Costs	Training on Duty or Non-Duty Hours
Agency pays the costs of training	Employee attends during duty hours
Agency pays the costs of training	Employee attends during non-duty hours
Agency pays some of the training costs. Employee pays the balance	Employee attends during duty hours
Agency pays some of the training employee pays the balance	Employee attends during non-duty hours
Employee pays all the training costs	Employee attends during duty hours
Agency reimburses part or all of costs	When course successfully completed (duty hours)
Employee pays all the training costs	Employee attends during non-duty hours
Agency reimburses part or all of costs	When course successfully completed (non-duty hours)
Employee pays all the training costs	Employee attends during duty hours

- Payment of Expenses to Obtain Professional Credentials - 5 U.S.C. 5757 allows agencies to use appropriated funds or funds otherwise available to the agency to pay for expenses for employees to obtain professional credentials, including expenses for professional accreditation. This authority allows the head of an agency the flexibility to pay for licenses and credentials that relate to the mission, goals and objectives of that agency. The exercise of this authority must be consistent with the merit system principles set forth in 5 U.S.C. 2301, as well as with any collective bargaining obligations. More information on paying for expenses to obtain professional credentials can be found on OPM's Fact Sheet on Certificate and Certification Programs.

- Paying for Academic Degrees - An agency may select and assign an employee to academic degree training and may pay or reimburse the cost of academic degree training from appropriated or other available funds, if such training contributes significantly to: (a) meeting identified agency training needs, (b) resolving an identified agency staffing problem; or (c) accomplishing goals in the strategic plan of the agency; is part of a planned employee development program aligned with the agency's strategic goals; and is both accredited and provided by a college or university that is itself accredited by a nationally recognized body, which is a regional, national, or international accrediting organization recognized by the U.S. Department of Education. This authority must be exercised in a manner consistent with the merit system principles set forth in paragraphs (2) and (7) of 5 U.S.C. 2301(b). (5 U.S.C. 4107)

- Allowing Employees to Accept Training or Reimbursement of Training Expenses from a Non-Profit Organization - A special provision of training law allows agencies to establish procedures where employees may accept reimbursement or waiver of tuition fees from non-profit organizations. Accepting free tuition or reimbursement of training expenses must not compromise the integrity of the employee or represent a payment for services rendered to the non-profit organization prior to the training. Prior approval from a designated high-level agency official is required, often following a consultation with, or review by, the designated agency ethics official. (5 U.S.C. 4111, 5 CFR 410.501)

4.   Training and Education-Related Travel Expenses

Travel, per diem, and transportation are training expenses governed by 5 U.S.C. 4109(a)(2)(A) and (B). The provisions in law that pertain to paying all or some of the costs of tuition and other training expenses apply to paying travel expenses. This means the agency decides which travel expenses it will pay for employees assigned to training. For example, an agency may:

- Pay the costs of training-related travel and per diem from program funds. (5 U.S.C. 4112, 5 CFR 410.304)
- Pay the costs of travel to a carrier in advance or advance an employee some or all of the cost of travel.
- Reimburse an employee for training-related travel expenses and/or share the costs of travel with an employee. (5 U.S.C. 4109(a)(2))
- Pay a reduced per diem rate to an employee in training status.
- Pay limited relocation expenses for an employee assigned to training for lengthy periods of time at the agency's discretion.

The following table illustrates the variety of arrangements that agencies and employees may use to share training-related travel expenses and accommodate schedules as well as the organization's and the employee's needs.

Paying Training-Related Travel Expenses	Training on Duty or Non-Duty Hours
Agency pays all the costs of travel	Employee attends during duty hours
Agency pays all the costs of travel	Employee attends during non-duty hours
Agency pays some of the travel costs. Employee pays the balance	Employee attends during duty hours
Agency pays some of the travel costs employee pays the balance	Employee attends during non-duty hours
Employee pays all the travel costs	Employee attends during non-duty hours
Agency reimburses part or all of the costs	When training is successfully completed

5.   Training and Education Unrelated to an Employee's Official Duties; Adjusting Employees' Work Schedules for Educational Purposes

Agencies may adjust an employee's normal work schedule for educational purposes. This authority allows the employee to take courses not related to his or her official duties. A special tour of duty is permissible if the following conditions are all met:

- The training will not appreciably interfere with work accomplishment.
- The agency incurs no additional personal services costs.
- Course completion will equip employee to more effectively work in the agency.
- The employee receives no premium pay while on the special tour of duty, even though premium pay would be otherwise payable. (5 CFR 610.122)

6.   Meetings Related to Agency Functions or To Improve Conduct of Agency Activities.

The meeting authority in 5 U.S.C. 4110 is separate from the training authority elsewhere in 5 U.S.C. chapter 41. The meeting authority is not subject to the other provisions of training law.

- Paying Meeting Expenses to Attend Meetings from Appropriated Funds. Professional meetings and conferences are valuable sources of information about innovative practices and current trends in various fields. Training law provides an exception to the prohibition in 5 U.S.C. 5946(1) on using appropriated funds to pay employee expenses for attending professional meetings. 5 U.S.C. 4110 allows an agency to use funds appropriated for travel expenses to pay for employees' expenses to attend meetings, if the meetings:

  o Concern functions or activities for which the appropriation is made, or
  o Will contribute to improved conduct, supervision, or management of the functions or activities. (5 U.S.C. 4110)

- Allowing Employees to Accept Reimbursement of Meeting Expenses from a Non-Profit Organization. A special provision of training law allows agencies to establish procedures under which employees may accept payment or reimbursement from a non-profit organization of travel, subsistence, and other expenses incident to attending meetings. Accepting meeting expenses must not compromise the integrity of the employee or represent a payment for services rendered to the non-profit organization prior to the meeting. Prior approval from a designated high-level agency official is required, often following a consultation with, or review by, the designated agency ethics official. (5 U.S.C. 4111)

7. Paying for Memberships in Professional Organizations

5 U.S.C. 5946(1) prohibits using appropriated funds to pay for individual employee memberships in professional associations and societies. However, there are several ways for an agency to obtain the professional, scientific, and technological information those associations provide their members. *See* GAO Red Book, Volume I, Chapter 4, p. 4-236-37. (So long as the membership inures to the benefit of the agency, use of appropriated funds may be considered a necessary expense.') For example, association membership is often included in registration fees for a conference or meeting. If the agency pays the registration fees, the employee's membership in the association is an incidental by-product of meeting attendance. In addition, agencies may purchase an organizational membership in the association or society. They may also purchase a membership for a specific agency position, such as the position of Medical Director. The incumbent in that position uses membership to improve the conduct, supervision, or management of his or her function.

As specified in 5 U.S.C. 4109, agencies may pay for membership fees that are a necessary cost directly related to the training itself, or if payment of the fee is a condition of participating in the training.

8. Continued Service Agreements to Protect the Government's Interest

A continued service agreement is an agreement an employee makes to continue to work for the Government for a pre-established length of time in exchange for Government-sponsored training or education. The service obligation begins when the training is completed. If the employee voluntarily leaves Government service before completing the service obligation, he or she must repay the Government all or some of the costs of the training (excluding salary). Agencies may require service agreements for training of long duration or of high cost. Agencies protect their investment and secure a period of service from an employee once the employee completes the training. (5 U.S.C. 4108) See OPM's fact sheet on Continuing Service Agreements for more information.

K. *LABOR-MANAGEMENT AND EMPLOYEE RELATIONS*

Partnership and Labor Relations (PLR) provides technical expertise, policy guidance, and professional development opportunities on employee and labor relations across the Federal government.

Contact: Partnership and Labor Relations, Labor Relations, at 202-606-2930 or email at PLR@opm.gov

1.   Labor Relations

Partnership and Labor Relations (PLR) supports the Director of the Office of Personnel Management as the principal policy advisor on labor-management relations. PLR assists agencies in working effectively with Federal labor organizations, which represent over 1.1 million Federal employees. PLR enhances Federal agencies' abilities to deal effectively with labor-management relations matters by conducting liaison activities with administration and agency officials. PLR regularly consults at the national level with labor organizations, agency managers and labor relations officials in the development of human resource policy and on Government rules, regulations, and binding directives affecting conditions of employment.

PLR supports effective labor-management relations which promote employee involvement, improved agency performance, and better service to the public. PLR is available to assist agency representatives in understanding their obligations, rights, and responsibilities under the Federal Service Labor-Management Relations Statute and preparing strategies for engaging the unionized workforce.

PLR facilitates and coordinates meetings and engagements of the National Council on Federal Labor Management Relations, established by Executive Order 13522. PLR also provides administrative support to the National Council for associated activities, including the maintenance of the LMR Council website.

2.   Poor Performance

PLR provides guidance to Federal agencies on taking performance-based actions. Agencies may take performance-based removal or demotion actions under 5 U.S.C. chapter 43, Performance Appraisal. Additionally, agencies may take performance-based removal, demotion, or suspension actions under 5 U.S.C. chapter 75, Adverse Actions. Each method has specific procedural and evidentiary requirements that must be met. (5 U.S.C. 4303 and 7513; 5 CFR parts 432 and 752)

Once an agency has issued a decision to remove an employee based solely on unacceptable performance, the employee may file a request for discontinued service retirement if the age and years-of-service requirements are met. However, an employee is not eligible for discontinued service retirement if the underlying reason for the removal is misconduct or delinquency, which can encompass willful refusal to perform. (5 U.S.C. 8336 and 8414)

When it is determined an employee is unable to perform his or her duties (including situations where the agency has issued a decision to remove the employee for poor performance) and a medical condition is causing the performance deficiency, the employee may seek OPM approval of disability retirement. If the employee is not eligible for disability retirement, he or she may be eligible for discontinued service retirement based on involuntary separation for medical reasons. (5 U.S.C. 8337 and 8451)

PLR and the Office of General Counsel review Merit Systems Protection Board (MSPB) decisions and arbitral awards on performance-based actions for consistency with civil service laws, rules and regulations and advise the OPM Director whether he should exercise his statutory authority to intervene or seek reconsideration of such decisions to obtain judicial review.

3.   Adverse Actions

PLR provides guidance to Federal agencies and employees on Adverse Actions. Most Federal agencies may suspend, demote, furlough, or remove employees under Chapter 75 of Title 5 for "such cause as will promote the efficiency of the service." (5 U.S.C. 7513; 5 CFR part 752) Such actions are called Adverse Actions. They are often based upon misconduct but may be undertaken based upon any cause that will promote the efficiency of the service. For example, these actions may also be based on unacceptable performance, a combination of both misconduct and performance, or non-disciplinary reasons such as medical inability to perform or furlough. PLR issues government-wide regulations at 5 CFR Part 752 which implement the statute.

PLR and the Office of General Counsel review MSPB decisions and arbitral awards on Adverse Actions for consistency with civil service laws, rules and regulations and advise the OPM Director whether he should exercise his statutory authority to intervene or seek reconsideration of such decisions to obtain judicial review.

L.   DISPUTE RESOLUTION

Across the Federal Government, agencies have found that alternative dispute resolution (ADR) often aids employees and managers in resolving internal disputes quickly and effectively, at the earliest possible time, and at the lowest possible level. This is especially important in the workplace, where festering disputes may distract an employee or manager from fulfilling essential work responsibilities. Use of ADR at the earliest possible stages of a workplace conflict can lead to early resolution that avoids costly litigation, conserves resources and contributes to a positive workplace environment. Agencies have considerable discretion in establishing ADR programs, within the constraints of applicable law. See 5 U.S.C. 571-584. Guidance and other information regarding ADR can be found at http://www.adr.gov/about-adr.html.

In addition, agencies have found that involvement in the ADR process often encourages supervisors to deal directly with the outcome of their or their subordinate's actions. In resolution of any dispute, agencies may use a variety of dispute resolution techniques to resolve employee disputes at the lowest possible level, thereby preventing costly and time-consuming formal processes and litigation. Such techniques can include various forms of ADR. Examples of ADR techniques are mediation, interest-based problem solving, binding arbitration, and facilitation.

PART III: HUMAN RESOURCES AUTHORITIES AND FLEXIBILITIES FOR THE SENIOR EXECUTIVE SERVICE

When the Civil Service Reform Act established the Senior Executive Service (SES) in 1978, a corporate SES culture was envisioned, and a distinct personnel system was mandated. The SES was designed to balance overall system uniformity with considerable agency flexibility for individual actions. Agency managers may exercise these authorities in accordance with law, regulations, and agency delegations. Contact Executive Resources and Employee Development at 202-606-8046.

A. POSITION MANAGEMENT

Within the overall allocation authorized by OPM, agencies have full responsibility for determining their executive resources priorities and establishing SES positions to meet these priorities. The number of positions established may exceed the number allocated, as long as the number of SES positions filled does not exceed the total agency allocation.

Agencies may:

- Establish and fill SES positions within their current allocation. (5 U.S.C. 3133; 5 CFR 214.202)

- Designate positions as General (G) or Career Reserved (CR) subject to regulatory criteria for CR designation. An agency must maintain a number of established CR positions equal to or greater than the career reserved minimum established by OPM for the agency. A career reserved position may only be filled by career SES appointment. (5 U.S.C. 3132(b)(1); 5 CFR 214.402)

B. STAFFING

The SES offers agency managers considerable flexibility in filling executive vacancies and resolving executive staffing problems.

1. Recruitment and Appointment

Agencies have authority to (and for some of these authorities must):

- Decide whether to fill a career reserved position competitively or noncompetitively (e.g., by reassignment, transfer, reinstatement, or appointment of a QRB-certified graduate of an SES candidate development program) and what recruitment methods will be used. (5 U.S.C. 3132, 3393, 3395(a), 3593; 5 CFR part 317, subparts E, F, G and I, 5 CFR 412.301(a))

- Decide whether to fill general positions by career, noncareer, limited term, or limited emergency appointment. (5 U.S.C. 3132(a)(4)-(7), 3133, 3134(d)-(e), 3393, 3394, 3395(b) and (c); 5 CFR part 317, subparts E, F, G, I and 5 CFR 412.301(a))

- Establish qualification standards for SES positions (mandatory). (5 U.S.C. 3392(a); 5 CFR part 317, subpart D)

- Establish Executive Resources Boards (ERBs) (mandatory) to conduct the merit staffing process leading to career SES appointments, including determining the area of consideration, establishing recruitment programs to locate highly qualified candidates, conducting the merit staffing process, evaluating qualifications, rating and ranking applicants, and making selection recommendations to the appointing authority. (5 U.S.C. 3393; 5 CFR part 317, subpart E)

- Determine whether candidates meet the qualifications for positions to be filled. (All SES appointees must meet the qualifications requirements of the position to which appointed, as determined in writing by the appointing authority; however, a Qualifications Review Board, established by OPM also must certify that proposed appointees meet executive qualifications for initial career appointment to the SES before the appointment may occur.) (5 U.S.C. 3393, 3394; 5 CFR 317.502)

- Make noncareer, limited term, or limited emergency appointments without competition after receiving OPM approval, except that prior OPM approval is not required for an SES limited term or limited emergency appointment made in accordance with the requirements of CFR 317.601(c) and within the agency's "pool" of delegated limited appointment authorities determined under that section. (5 U.S.C. 3134, 3394; 5 CFR 317, subpart F)

- Supplement USAJOBS and other agency recruiting efforts by using commercial recruiting firms and nonprofit employment services to recruit for vacancies where such use is likely to provide well-qualified candidates who otherwise would not be available. (5 CFR part 300, subpart D)

2.   Short-Term Staffing Needs

Agencies may:

- Make an SES limited term appointment (up to 3 years) of an individual serving under a career or career-type appointment (outside the SES) to an SES General position established for temporary project-type work within the "pool" of SES limited authorities available to the agency under 5 CFR 317.601(c), or request OPM approval for an SES limited term appointment for an individual who is not eligible under that provision. (5 U.S.C. 3132(a)(5), 3394, 3395; 5 CFR 317, subpart F)

- Make an SES limited emergency appointment (up to 18 months) of an individual serving under a career or career-type appointment (outside the SES) to an SES General position established to meet a bona-fide, unanticipated, urgent need within the "pool" of SES limited authorities available to the agency under 5 CFR 317.601(c), or request OPM approval for an SES limited emergency appointment for an individual who is not eligible under that provision. (5 U.S.C. 3132(a)(6), 3394, 3395; 5 CFR 317, subpart F)

- Detail a non-SES employee to an SES position in increments of 120 days, with competition required for any time beyond 240 days. (Prior OPM approval is also required if the detail beyond 240 days is to an SES position supervising other SES positions). Detail an SES member to a non-SES position or to unclassified duties in increments of 120 days, with

OPM approval required for any time beyond 240 days. Detail SES members to other SES positions in increments of 120 days. (5 U.S.C. 3341; 5 CFR 317.903)

3.   Lateral Movement

Agencies may:

- Reassign career appointees to any SES position in the same agency for which qualified after 15 day advance written notice if within commuting area, or after consultation and 60 day advance written notice if outside the commuting area. (5 U.S.C.3395(a); 5 CFR 317.901)

- Reassign noncareer appointees to any SES General position in the same agency for which qualified, with prior OPM approval. (5 U.S.C. 3395(d)(1); 5 CFR 317.604)

- Reassign a limited or limited emergency appointee to an SES General position in the same agency that meets the same criteria under which the original appointment was made, without prior OPM approval. (5 U.S.C. 3395(b); 5 CFR 317.604)

- Transfer a career appointee to an SES position for which qualified in another agency, with the consent of the gaining agency and the employee. (5 U.S.C. 3395(a)(1); 5 CFR 317.902)

- Transfer noncareer appointees to any SES General position for which qualified in another agency, with approval of the gaining agency and OPM. (5 U.S.C. 3395(d)(2); 5 CFR 317.902)

- Appoint eligible SES equivalent executives serving in an agency with an interchange agreement to SES positions noncompetitively. (An executive must meet the qualifications of the position.) (5 CFR parts 6.7 and 214.204)

Exception: A career appointee may not be involuntarily reassigned within 120 days of the appointment of a new agency head or a new noncareer supervisor who has authority to make an initial appraisal of the appointee's performance. (5 U.S.C. 3395(e); 5 CFR 317.901)

C.   COMPENSATION

Agencies have discretionary authority to set pay and to provide additional compensation to meet recruitment, relocation, and retention needs. Agencies should ensure that any compensation flexibilities are used judiciously and in accordance with applicable law, regulations, agency policy, and budgetary limitations. Under 5 U.S.C. 5307, most additional payments are subject to the limitation that aggregate pay may not exceed the rate for Executive Level I (for agency performance appraisal systems that are not certified), or the compensation payable to the Vice President under 3 U.S.C. 104 (for agency performance appraisal systems that are certified). (5 U.S.C. 5307 and 5 CFR part 530, subpart B)

1.   Agency-Based Compensation Flexibilities

Additional information is available at http://www.opm.gov/policy-data-oversight/senior-executive-service/performance/.

Agencies may:

- Set an SES member's rate of basic pay at any rate within the SES rate range. The minimum rate of the SES rate range is equivalent to the minimum rate of basic pay for senior-level employees (i.e., 120 percent of the rate for GS-15, step 1). The maximum rate of the SES rate range is equivalent to level III of the Executive Schedule for senior executives covered by a performance appraisal system not certified, or the rate for level II of the Executive Schedule for senior executives covered by a certified performance appraisal system. An agency may not adjust an SES member's rate of basic pay more than once during any 12-month period, except in limited situations as prescribed by OPM regulations and guidance.

- Re-employ annuitants on a temporary basis without salary off-set under certain specified circumstances, without OPM approval. (5 U.S.C. 8344(l) and 8468(i)) See discussion in earlier section on re-employing annuitants without salary offset at Staffing the Organization: Alternative Staffing Options.

- Pay recruitment incentives for new appointees and relocation incentives for current employees who move to a different geographic area (excluding non-career SES members), when a position is likely to be difficult to fill in the absence of an incentive. Agencies should ensure that any compensation flexibilities are used judiciously and in accordance with applicable law, regulations, agency policy, and budgetary limitations. (5 U.S.C. 5753; 5 CFR part 575, subparts A and B)

- Pay retention incentives to an employee (excluding a non-career SES member), when (1) unusually high or unique qualifications of the individual, or a special need of the agency makes it essential to retain an individual who would be likely to leave the Federal service in the absence of an incentive, or (2) the agency has a special need for the employee's services that makes it essential to retain the employee in his or her current position during a period of time before the closure or relocation of the employee's office, facility, activity, or organization and the employee would be likely to leave for a different position in the Federal service in the absence of a retention incentive. Agencies should ensure that any compensation flexibilities are used judiciously and in accordance with applicable law, regulations, agency policy, and budgetary limitations. (5 U.S.C. 5754; 5 CFR part 575, subpart C)

- Pay travel expenses of candidates for SES positions for pre-employment interviews requested by the agency. (5 U.S.C. 5752; 5 CFR part 572)

- Pay travel and transportation expenses for new appointees to the first post of duty. (The General Services Administration (GSA) issues implementation regulations as part of Federal Travel Regulations.) (5 U.S.C. 5723; 5 CFR part 572)

- Provide an advance in pay up to two pay periods, to any individual newly appointed in the agency. (5 U.S.C. 5524a; 5 CFR part 550, subpart B)

- Pay travel and transportation expenses for career appointees for "last move home." If reassigned or transferred geographically (when eligible for optional or discontinued service retirement or within 5 years of eligibility for optional retirement), senior executives are entitled to moving expenses at retirement. (GSA issues implementation regulations as part of Federal Travel Regulations.) (5 U.S.C. 5724)

- Authorize flexible or compressed work schedules under an alternative work schedule (AWS) for SES members. (SES members may not accumulate credit hours under AWS and are not entitled to premium pay (e.g. overtime and comp time).) (5 U.S.C. chapter 61, subchapter II; 5 CFR part 610, subpart D)

- Authorize student loan repayments in accordance with the agency's student loan repayment plan. (5 U.S.C. 5379 and 5 CFR part 537)

2. Compensation Flexibilities Available with OPM and/or OMB Approval

Agencies may:

- Request critical position pay authority from OPM, in consultation with OMB, permitting the agency to set basic pay up to the rate for level I of the Executive Schedule, where necessary to enable the agency to recruit or retain an exceptionally well qualified individual for a position that requires expertise of an extremely high level in a scientific, technical, professional, or administrative field, and is critical to the accomplishment of an important agency mission. Critical pay may be granted only to the extent necessary to recruit or retain an individual who is exceptionally well qualified for the position. A rate in excess of level I may only be established in rare circumstances with the written approval of the President. (5 U.S.C. 5377 and 5 CFR part 535)

- Request OPM to waive salary offset for civilian re-employed annuitants on a case-by-case basis, for employees in positions for which there is exceptional difficulty in recruiting or retaining a qualified employee, or to meet an emergency hiring need as specified in law. An agency may also ask OPM to delegate authority to approve reemployment without reduction or termination of annuity in emergencies or other unusual circumstances. These waivers are intended to be rare exceptions, used only in the most unusual circumstances. (5 U.S.C. 8344(i) and 8468(f); 5 CFR part 553, subpart B)

- Pay recruitment, relocation, or retention incentives, in excess of the regular limitations upon OPM approval based on a critical agency need. Agencies should ensure that any compensation flexibilities are used judiciously and in accordance with applicable law, regulations, agency policy, and budgetary limitations. (5 U.S.C. 5753 and 5754; 5 CFR part 575, subparts A, B, and C)

D. PERFORMANCE MANAGEMENT

Performance management in the SES provides for systematically assessing individual executive performance including, as appropriate, holding executives accountable for achieving organizational performance against agency goals and objectives, establishing accountability for achieving results, as appropriate, and linking performance with decisions about pay, awards, and other personnel actions.

1. Performance Planning and Appraisal Certification for Pay Purposes

Agencies must:

- Establish performance management policies and systems to plan for and appraise individual performance of senior executives in a manner informed by the performance of their organizations. Once OPM approves an agency performance appraisal system, the agency is responsible for its SES performance management. (5 U.S.C. 4312; 5 CFR part 430, subpart C)

- Implement performance appraisal including:
    1. Identifying, establishing, and communicating performance elements and requirements for individual executives;
    2. Monitoring progress and providing feedback to executives;
    3. Appraising performance against requirements annually (with provision for shortening an executive's appraisal period when appropriate); and
    4. Establishing Performance Review Boards to review initial summary ratings and make recommendations to the agency head on annual summary ratings and bonuses. (5 U.S.C. chapter 43, subchapter II; 5 CFR part 430, subpart C)

Obtain certification of the agency's SES performance appraisal system by OPM, with OMB concurrence, based upon criteria specified in regulation, if the agency wants authority to pay executives rates of basic pay up to level II of the Executive Schedule, rather than the level III maximum that otherwise applies, and to apply a higher aggregate pay cap, i.e., the compensation payable to the Vice President, rather than level I of the Executive Schedule, which otherwise applies. (5 U.S.C. 5307(d) and 5382; 5 CFR part 430, subpart D)

Agency head decisions on ratings, bonuses, or removals from the SES based on ratings are not subject to appeal to a third party such as the Merit Systems Protection Board. A non-probationary career appointee who is being removed from the SES is entitled to an informal hearing before MSPB, which need not delay removal.) (5 U.S.C. 3592(a)(2), 4312(d), and 5384(b)(2); 5 CFR part 359 subpart E; 5 CFR 430.308(d) and (f))

Exception: Performance ratings for career appointees may not be made within 120 days after the beginning of a new Presidential administration. (5 U.S.C. 4314(b))

2.   Awards and Recognition

Agencies may:

- Pay annual lump sum performance awards (bonuses) to SES career members, after considering the agency Performance Review Board recommendations. Awards may be between 5 percent and 20 percent of their basic pay. A bonus may not be less than 5 percent or more than 20 percent of the executive's rate of basic pay. The number of bonuses agency-wide is not restricted but the total amount of bonuses may not exceed the greater of—1) 10 percent of the aggregate amount of basic pay paid to agency career executives, or 2) 20 percent of the average of the annual rates of basic pay paid to agency career executives, during the preceding fiscal year. (5 U.S.C. 5384; 5 CFR 534.405)

- Pay awards for suggestions, inventions, superior accomplishment, productivity gain, or special acts or service. Gain-sharing programs may also be used where organizational characteristics permit. Agencies may grant up to $10,000 without OPM approval; up to $25,000 with OPM approval; and in excess of $25,000 with Presidential approval. (The Department of Defense and the Internal Revenue Service do not require OPM approval for awards up to $25,000, but the President must approve awards over $25,000 after review and approval by OPM.) Award payments are subject to the aggregate limitation on total pay equal to the rate of pay for Executive Level I. For members of the Senior Executive Service, this aggregate limitation on total pay is equal to the rate of the Vice President's salary when they are covered by a certified performance appraisal system. (5 U.S.C. chapter 45; 5 CFR part 451 and 5 U.S.C. 5307(d); 5 CFR part 530, subpart B; and 5 CFR part 430, subpart D)

- Nominate career executives for Presidential Rank Awards for sustained accomplishment over an extended period. Distinguished Executives receive 35 percent of annual basic pay; Meritorious Executives receive 20 percent of annual basic pay. (5 U.S.C. 4507; 5 CFR 451, subpart C)

- Grant time off without charge to leave or loss of pay, as an incentive. (5 U.S.C. 4502(e); 5 CFR 451.104(a))

3.   Performance Development and Training

Agencies are responsible for:

- Establishing programs for the systematic development of candidates for the SES and for the continuing development of senior executives. (5 U.S.C. 3396; 5 CFR part 412)

- Providing any training that will assist in achieving the agency's mission and performance goals, with no requirement that training be directly related to "official duties." (5 U.S.C. 4103)

- Training employees for placement in another agency, when such training is in the interest of the Government. (5 U.S.C. 4103)

- Taking full advantage of available training sources with no distinction made between Government and non-Government sources. (5 U.S.C. 4105)

- Determining when a "continued service agreement" with an employee is appropriate and applying it to such training as is necessary to protect the Government's investment. (5 U.S.C. 4108; 5 CFR 410.309)

An agency may:

- Grant a sabbatical to a career SES member not to exceed 11 months during any 10-year period for study or uncompensated work experience contributing to the employee's development and effectiveness. The employee retains salary and benefits, and the agency may grant travel and per diem costs. (5 U.S.C. 3396(c))

4.   Poor Performance

Agencies have the authority to

- Take performance-based reassignment or removal actions under 5 U.S.C. chapter 43, subchapter II, Performance Appraisal in the SES. Removal actions have specific procedural and documentation requirements that must be met. After removal from the SES, most career appointees will have placement rights to positions at grade 15 or above with SES saved pay. (5 U.S.C. 3592(a), 3594, 4314(b); 5 CFR part 359, subparts E and G).

- Rather than remove a career appointee who receives a single unsatisfactory rating, reassign the appointee to another SES position and provide assistance in improving performance (e.g., counseling, training, or closer supervision). (5 U.S.C. 4314(b); 5 CFR 430.306(a) and 430.309)

- Remove a probationary career appointee from the SES for unacceptable performance, with a one-day advance written notice. After removal, a probationer who was appointed to the SES from a career or career-conditional appointment (or an appointment of equivalent tenure) will have placement rights to a position at grade 15 or above with SES saved pay. (5 U.S.C. 3592(a), 3594, 4314; 5 CFR part 359, subparts D and G)

- Remove a non-probationary career appointee from the SES for unacceptable performance, with a 30-day advance written notice. A career appointee may not appeal a removal action but is entitled to an informal hearing before the MSPB upon request, which shall not give the career appointee a right to initiate an appeal and need not delay the removal date. (5 U.S.C. 3592(a), 4314(b); 5 CFR part 359, subpart E)

- Remove a noncareer, limited term, or limited emergency appointee from the SES for unacceptable performance, with a one-day advance written notice. (5 U.S.C. 3592(c), 4314; 5 CFR part 359, subpart I)

E.   *OTHER SES REMOVAL ACTIONS*

Agencies have the authority to remove executives from the SES for a variety of reasons in addition to unacceptable performance, such as misconduct and reduction in force. Each method has specific procedural and evidentiary requirements that must be met. Some executives may have placement rights to grade 15 positions.

Agencies may:

- Remove a career appointee at any time during the probationary period, with a one-day written notice. A probationer who was appointed to the SES from a career or career-conditional appointment (or an appointment of equivalent tenure) will have placement rights to a grade 15 or above with SES saved pay, if removed for reasons other than misconduct, neglect of duty, malfeasance or other disciplinary reasons under 5 CFR 359.403, 5 CFR 359.404, or part 752, sub-part F of the OPM regulations. If removal is for cause as defined by 5 U.S.C. 7543, a probationer who was covered by 5 U.S.C. chapter 75, subchapter II prior to SES appointment has the same procedural protections as a non-probationary career appointee but removal is from the civil service and not just from the SES. (5 U.S.C. 3592, 3594, 5 U.S.C. chapter 75, subchapter V; 5 CFR part 359, subparts D and G, 5 CFR part 752, subpart F)

- Remove non-probationary career appointees for cause, as defined by 5 U.S.C. 7543 (e.g., misconduct, neglect of duty, malfeasance, or failure to accept a directed reassignment or to accompany a position in a transfer of function), with a 30-day advance written notice. Removal is from the civil service and not just from the SES. (An agency also has authority to suspend a non-probationary career appointee for more than 14 days under the same provisions.) (5 U.S.C. chapter 75, subchapter V; 5 CFR part 752, subpart F)

- Remove career executives through SES reduction-in-force (SES RIF) based on competitive procedures. A non-probationer can be removed by SES RIF only if there are no vacant SES positions in the agency for which the executive is qualified and OPM is unable to place the executive in another agency during the 45-day priority placement period. Probationers identified for SES RIF through competitive procedures can be removed with a one-day notice. All non-probationary career appointees and probationary career appointees who were appointed from a career or career-conditional appointment (or an appointment of equivalent tenure) will have placement rights to a position at grade 15 or above with SES saved pay upon removal. A career appointee, including a probationer, may appeal to MSPB whether the SES RIF complied with competitive procedures. (5 U.S.C. 3594, 3595; 5 CFR part 359, subparts D, F and G)

- Remove a noncareer, limited term or limited emergency appointees at any time, with a one-day written notice, except that if the proposed removal is for cause as defined in 5 U.S.C.

7543, an SES limited term or limited emergency appointee who was covered by 5 U.S.C. chapter 75, subchapter II, immediately before the SES appointment has the same procedural protections that apply to a non-probationary career appointee. (5 U.S.C. 3592(c), 7541; 5 CFR part 359, subpart I; 5 CFR part 752, subpart F)

- Remove re-employed annuitants at any time, with a one-day written notice. (5 CFR part 359, subpart I)

Exception: During the 120-day period following appointment of a new agency head or a new noncareer supervisor with removal authority, career appointees in the SES may not be removed for performance reasons, except when: 1) removal is under 5 U.S.C. 4314(b)(3) and based on an unsatisfactory rating given before the appointment, 2) removal of a probationer for misconduct, neglect of duty, malfeasance or other disciplinary reasons under 5 CFR 359.403, 5 CFR 359.404, or part 752, sub-part F of the OPM regulations is initiated under 5 CFR part 359, subpart D before the appointment, or 3) removal of a probationer for misconduct, neglect of duty, malfeasance or other disciplinary reasons under 5 CFR 359.403, 5 CFR 359.404, or part 752, sub-part F of the OPM regulations is initiated under 5 CFR part 359, subpart D after the appointment but certain aggravating circumstances apply. (Note that: 1) The restriction described here does not apply to an adverse action removal under 5 U.S.C. chapter 75, subchapter V; and 2) if a career appointee's probationary period expires during the 120 restriction on removal, any subsequent removal action must be taken under the rules that apply to a nonprobationary career appointee.) (5 U.S.C. 3592(b); 5 CFR part 359, subparts D and E, esp. 359.406(c) and 359.503 (c)).